canning
in the
modern
kitchen

canning in the modern kitchen

More Than 100 Recipes for Canning and Cooking Fruits, Vegetables, and Meats

Jamie DeMent

RODALE

RODALE and the Plant colophon are registered trademarks of
Penguin Random House LLC.

Library of Congress Cataloging-in-Publication Data is available.
ISBN 978-1-63565-203-1
Ebook ISBN 978-1-63565-204-8

Printed in China

Book design by Yeon Kim
Photographs by Mitch Mandel
Food styling by Laura Kinsey Dolph
Prop styling by Stephanie Hanes

10 9 8 7 6 5 4 3 2 1
First Edition

To my mama, nanny, grandma, and Gigi: Y'all are with me with every jar I fill and every step I take.

contents

introduction

TODAY I'M A FARMER, RESTAURATEUR, AND WRITER. My life revolves around food—growing it, selling it, writing about it. Our farm is an idyllic spot in the heart of North Carolina, on the banks of the Eno River. We raise heirloom produce and heritage breed pasture-raised meats with a wonderful team of folks who work and live on our farm. We work together, live together, and do a lot of eating and celebrating together. The meals we enjoy are built around what we grow and would not be possible without preserving food from one season to another.

Luckily, I was born and raised in North Carolina. My family on both sides is full of strong-minded, colorful women who loved to cook—grandmothers, great-aunts, cousins, friends closer than cousins—all women who showed their love through their cooking. Some of my earliest memories are being in my grandma's "canning kitchen" three generations deep, tiny baby hands next to arthritic fingers stuffing okra into jars and stirring big, steaming pots of vegetables. There was always a medley of voices of all those women, who taught me not just to cook but to love and nurture. I can stop almost any moment of any day and bring back memories of that warm kitchen and feel loved and protected all over again.

I use techniques from that kitchen in my farm kitchen every year. I make sauces, pestos, compotes, jams, and jellies to carry treasured flavors from season to season. And then I use my preserved food to feed our farm family and friends for the rest of the year.

If you are new to canning and feel anxious about the processes, never fear: *Canning in the Modern Kitchen* will walk you through the basics and start you with tasty but classic canning treats. If you're an experienced canner, you'll find plenty of flavorful recipes that will expand your repertoire and enrich your pantry.

Every recipe has been tested in my kitchen—indeed, many are family favorites that I rely on year after year to add zest and delight to the dinner table. As you'll see, canning can be fun as well as delicious! So let's get started by looking at the most common home-canning methods.

the processes

BOILING-WATER-BATH CANNING

This is the most basic and safest way to can high-acid fruits and vegetables. This will be your go-to method for many pickles and tomato-based sauces. It's my favorite way to can and the process I learned first. I recommend starting with this process if you have never canned before. Always make sure to fully read your recipe and process before getting started to make sure you have everything you need on hand.

EQUIPMENT

Recipe

Glass preserving jars, lids, and
   bands (new lids only!)

Large pot (for heating jars)

Wooden spoon

Blanching bag or basket

Spice bag or cheesecloth

Large stockpot or canning pot with lid

Canning rack

Small saucepan or kettle

Jar lifter or heavy-duty tongs

Hot-jar grip/handler or clean,
   sturdy potholders

Ladle

Funnel

Towel

PROCESS

1   Get everything ready: *Read through your recipe and instructions* and assemble all your equipment and recipe ingredients. Follow the guidelines in each recipe for the recipe preparation, jar size, preserving method, and processing time.

2   Wash the canning jars, lids, and bands in hot, soapy water. Rinse well. Dry the bands.

3   The jars need to be hot when they are filled, so heat them in a large pot filled halfway with water. The water should be hot, but not boiling. Keep the jars in the hot water until you are ready to use them. Alternatively, you

could prepare the jars by washing them on high heat in the dishwasher. You'll just have to keep opening and closing the dishwasher as you fill jars.

4 Prepare the ingredients (cut, cook, etc.) according to the recipe, using the wooden spoon, blanching bag or basket, and/or spice bag or cheese-cloth as directed by the recipe.

5 Get a big pot—a large stockpot or one of those giant speckled enameled pots sold at the hardware store every summer. Place an appropriately sized canning rack in the bottom of the pot to keep jars from sitting directly on the pan bottom. Fill the pot with the appropriate amount of water (see the next paragraph) and begin heating it on the stovetop over high heat.

6 Boiling-water-bath canning requires 1" to 2" of water *above* the tops of jars, so try to gauge how much water you need by how much water is going to be displaced when you put your full jars in the water. It is always a good idea to have an additional small pan or kettle of water boiling on the stove just in case you need to top off the water level in the canner.

7 Very carefully, set up your hot, clean jars. You can protect your fingers by moving the jars with a jar lifter or clean potholders. Use a ladle and funnel to fill each jar (the funnel keeps your jar rims clean, and that's necessary for a good seal). After a jar is filled, tap it gently on the counter to remove air bubbles. Clean rims and secure lids. Repeat this process until all your jars are filled.

8 Bring the canning pot to a rolling boil. Use a jar lifter or heavy-duty tongs to carefully lower the filled jars into the boiling water. The jars should be covered by 1" to 2" of water. Add additional boiling water, if needed (this is where the extra pan of heated water comes in handy). If you add more water, pour it between the jars, not directly on them. Cover the canning pot with its lid, and bring the water back to a boil.

9 When the water comes to a rolling boil again, start to count the process-ing time as specified by your recipe. Reduce the heat slightly and boil gently for the time recommended for the food being processed. Be sure to adjust for altitude by using the handy chart on page 24.

introduction

10 When the cooking time is up, turn off the heat and let the water cool. When the jars have cooled for 4 to 5 minutes, remove them from the canner with the jar lifter or tongs and sit them upright on a towel in a draft-free area. Leave them alone overnight (at least 12 hours).

11

11 After 24 hours, check your lids to make sure they sealed completely. They should not flex up and down when you press in the middle of the lid. Remove the bands and try to lift the lids with gentle finger pressure. You're not actually trying to get the lid off—just testing it. If it stays on, the seal is good. If the jars haven't sealed, it's usually because something got between the lid and the edge of the jar. You can try cleaning off the top of the jar, reheating the contents, and sterilizing the rims again to reprocess, or you can put those jars in the refrigerator and use within the week. Label your jars and store them in a cool, dark place. Get ready to enjoy months of good eating!

PRESSURE CANNING

Do not be afraid of pressure canning! Once you get the knack of it, you'll find that it is not much more difficult than the boiling-water-bath option. And it's the only way to can low-acid foods, so you need to learn it anyway! Low-acid foods (vegetables, soups, stews, stocks, broths, juices, and meats) really can be simple to preserve. They just require more heat and careful handling to prevent the risk of botulism. Low-acid foods absolutely have to be heated and processed at a temperature of 240°F for a specified amount of time (depending on what you're preserving). Different ingredients take different amounts of time at different altitudes. Pressure canning is the only way to get the heat you need. Each recipe in this book includes the processing time appropriate for that recipe.

If you're doing this for the first time, read the instructions that came with your pressure canner closely. Pressure canners all work on the same principles, but each one is different, so pay close attention to the manufacturer's notes. Also, read all the way through your recipe and have all ingredients and equipment ready before you get started. The process will not wait on you, so be well prepared.

EQUIPMENT

Recipe

Glass preserving jars, lids, and bands (new lids only!)

Large pot (for heating jars)

Wooden spoon

Blanching bag or basket

Spice bag or cheesecloth

Pressure canner

Ladle

Funnel

Jar lifter or heavy-duty tongs

Hot-jar grip/handler or clean, sturdy potholders

PROCESS

1 Get everything ready: *Read through your recipe and instructions* and assemble all your equipment and recipe ingredients. Follow the guidelines in each recipe for the recipe preparation, jar size, preserving method, and processing time.

2 Wash the canning jars, lids, and bands in hot, soapy water. Rinse well. Dry the bands.

3 The jars need to be hot when they are filled, so heat them in a large pot filled halfway with water. The water

introduction

should be hot, but not boiling. Keep the jars in the hot water until you are ready to use them. Alternatively, you could prepare the jars by washing them on high heat in the dishwasher. You'll just have to keep opening and closing the dishwasher as you fill jars.

4 Prepare the ingredients (cut, cook, etc.) according to the recipe, using the wooden spoon, blanching bag or basket, and/or spice bag or cheese-cloth as directed by the recipe.

5 Fill the pressure canner with 2" to 3" of water and place on the stove top over medium-high heat. Bring to a simmer. Keep the water at a simmer until all the jars are filled and placed in the canner. Follow the manufac-turer's instructions for using the canner.

6 Very carefully, set up your hot, clean jars. You can protect your fingers by moving the jars with a jar lifter or clean potholders. Use a ladle and funnel to fill each jar (the funnel keeps your jar rims clean, and that's necessary for a good seal). After a jar is filled, tap it gently on the counter to remove air bubbles. Repeat this process until all your jars are filled.

7 Clean the rims and threads of each jar using a clean, damp cloth to remove any food residue. Place a lid securely on each jar and secure the lid with a band, just until it's finger tight. You want room for bubbles to escape. Place the filled jars in the canner using the jar lifter or tongs, then make sure the water is at the suggested height—usually 2" to 3", but canners can vary, so review your canner's instructions. If you have extra jars left when the canner is full, save them and process in another batch.

8 Lock the lid of the canner in place, leaving the vent pipe open. Turn the heat to medium–high and allow steam to escape through the vent pipe. When there is a steady stream of steam, leave the vent open for 10 more minutes to get all the air out of the canner. Then close the vent with the weight according to the manufacturer's instructions and gradually adjust the heat to achieve the recommended pounds of pressure.

9 Leave the jars in the canner, adjusting the heat as necessary to maintain pressure, for the processing time

introduction

indicated in your recipe. Be sure to adjust for altitude by using the handy chart on page 24.

10 When you've processed the jars to the set time, start the cooldown process. Do not remove the vent weight until the canner has cooled! In general, follow the manufacturer's instructions for opening. Carefully remove the canner from the stovetop. Let the canner stand undisturbed until the interior pressure returns to zero—at least 10 minutes. When you are ready, remove the vent weight and unlock the lid, tilting the canner carefully away from you. Wait 10 more minutes to allow the jars to begin to cool before you try to move them.

11 When the jars have cooled some, remove them from the canner and sit them upright on a towel in a draft-free area. Leave them alone overnight (at least 12 hours).

12 Finally, check your lids to make sure they sealed. They should not flex up and down when you press in the middle of the lid. Remove the bands and try to lift the lids with gentle finger pressure. You're not actually trying to get the lid off—just testing it. If it stays on, the seal is good. If the lid comes off, refrigerate the contents and use within a week. Label your jars with the recipe name and date, and store them in a cool, dark place. Get ready to enjoy months of good eating!

canning
charts

Times and pressure information given in the recipes are for elevations of 1,000 feet above sea level or less. If you live higher than that elevation, water will boil at temperatures lower than 212°F, so use the following charts to make adjustments for both boiling-water-bath canning and pressure canning.

ALTITUDE ADJUSTMENT FOR BOILING-WATER-BATH CANNING	
ALTITUDE IN FEET	INCREASE PROCESSING TIME
1001-3000	5 minutes
3001-6000	10 minutes
6001-8000	15 minutes
8001-10,000	20 minutes

ALTITUDE ADJUSTMENT FOR PRESSURE CANNING		
ALTITUDE IN FEET	DIAL GAUGE CANNER	WEIGHTED GAUGE CANNER
0-1000	10	10
1001-2000	11	15
2001-4000	12	15
4001-6000	13	15
6001-8000	14	15
8001-10,000	15	15

This chart is a general guide for preserving foods based on their acidity. High-acid foods are safe to be canned using the water bath process; foods with lower acid require pressure canning. In some cases, adding lemon juice or vinegar can raise the acidity of low-acid foods to make them safe to can using the water bath method.

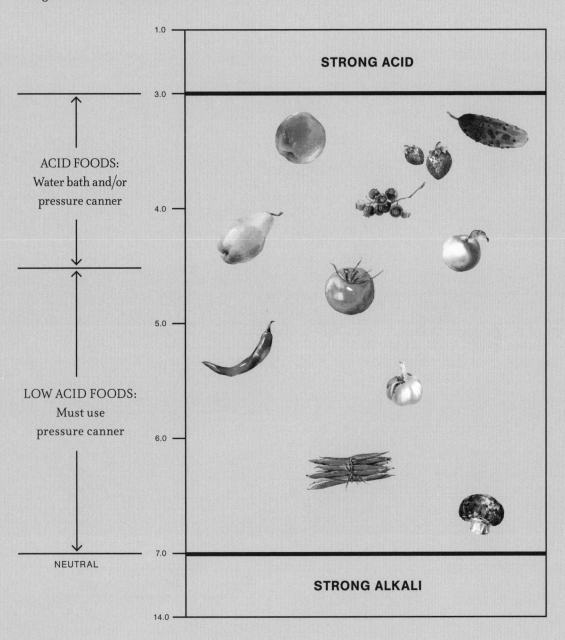

STRONG ACID

ACID FOODS:
Water bath and/or
pressure canner

LOW ACID FOODS:
Must use
pressure canner

NEUTRAL

STRONG ALKALI

1.0
3.0
4.0
5.0
6.0
7.0
14.0

CHAPTER 1
basic fruits and vegetables

Let's begin with the basics.

There are some things that are so delicious in their natural state that you want to eat them year-round just that way—in their most simple form. The recipes in this section preserve fruits and vegetables in their purest forms and give us a great place to start learning about canning!

peaches

I'm starting with peaches because they are my single most favorite thing to eat canned—straight out of the jar. They are great as a snack alone or as a wonderful addition to salads and desserts. I make them in pint jars to keep myself from eating a whole quart in one sitting! This recipe uses fruit juice instead of sugar as a base because the canned peaches will be more versatile for later use if they are less sweet. The best ripe peaches, depending on where you live, tend to be available between June and August.

MAKES 7–8 PINTS

Get your boiling-water-bath canning equipment ready and have your jars sterilized and ready.

8 pounds fresh peaches

3 tablespoons fresh lemon juice

$\frac{1}{2}$ gallon white grape juice

1. Fill a large bowl with ice water and set it to the side. Bring a large pot of water to a boil. Drop the peaches into the boiling water, making sure they are all submerged. (Work in batches, if necessary.) Blanch the peaches for about 3 minutes, or until you can easily peel the skin off a cooled peach by hand. Using a slotted spoon, carefully transfer the peaches to the ice water. Let them cool in the water for 1 minute.

2. Using your fingers, quickly remove the skins from all the peaches. Cut the peaches in half, remove the pits, and put the halves in another large bowl. Add the lemon juice and gently stir to evenly coat the peaches (this prevents them from turning brown).

3. In a large stockpot, bring the grape juice to a boil. While the juice is heating, carefully pack the peach halves into hot, sterilized jars, leaving about 1" of headspace.

4. Once the juice has reached a rolling boil, carefully ladle or pour the hot juice over the peaches, leaving $\frac{1}{2}$" of headspace. Gently tap the jars to make sure all the peaches are completely surrounded by liquid and there are no air bubbles. Add more hot juice now if needed.

5. Wipe the rim of each jar carefully with a clean towel to ensure a good seal, and carefully place the lids and rims on.

6. Follow your boiling-water-bath canning process and process for 25 minutes, adjusting for altitude based on the chart on page 24.

basic fruits and vegetables

pears

We have a pear tree, an old Bartlett variety, that produces more fruit than we can keep up with, so I preserve the fruit as it ripens. The pears can always be baked or frozen, but canning lets you keep some of that fresh pear crunch. This recipe doesn't use sugar, so it gives you more flexibility in how you can use your preserved pears in later recipes—as a savory salad, or dinner additions, or sweet pie fillings.

MAKES 4 PINTS

Get your boiling-water-bath canning equipment ready and have your jars sterilized and ready.

6 pounds firm, ripe pears
3 tablespoons fresh lemon juice

1. Wash, peel, core, and cut the pears into halves or quarters and place in a large bowl. Add the lemon juice and gently stir to evenly coat. Let the pears soak for 2 to 3 minutes.
2. Meanwhile, bring a large pot of water to a boil.
3. Pack the pears into hot, sterilized jars. Carefully pour the boiling water over the pears, leaving 1/2" of headspace. Gently tap the jars to make sure all the pears are completely surrounded by liquid and there are no air bubbles.

4. Wipe the rim of each jar carefully with a clean towel to ensure a good seal, and carefully place the lids and rims on.
5. Follow your boiling-water-bath canning process and process for 25 minutes, adjusting for altitude based on the chart on page 24.

honeyed cherries

We love cherries at our house! We eat them fresh as long as we can and put them up for later use in everything from desserts to duck potpie. Pitting the cherries will take a while, but it's worth every minute. The recipe works with sweet and tart cherries.

MAKES 6 PINTS

Get your boiling-water-bath canning equipment ready and have your jars sterilized and ready.

2 quarts fresh cherries

3 tablespoons fresh lemon juice

2 cups honey

4 cups water

1. Wash and pit the cherries and place in a large bowl. Add the lemon juice and gently stir to coat. Set the cherries aside to soak.

2. Meanwhile, in a large pot over medium-high heat, bring the honey and water to a boil. Cook over medium heat for 8 to 10 minutes, or until a syrup forms.

3. Pack the cherries into hot, sterilized jars. Carefully pour the boiling syrup over the cherries, leaving $1/2$" of headspace. Gently tap the jars to make sure all the cherries are completely surrounded by liquid and there are no air bubbles. Add more syrup now, if needed.

4. Wipe the rim of each jar carefully with a clean towel to ensure a good seal, and carefully place the lids and rims on.

5. Follow your boiling-water-bath canning process and process for 25 minutes, adjusting for altitude based on the chart on page 24.

berries

Who doesn't want to keep the flavors of berries around all year long? Berries are a bit of a different beast, though, and need a little more sugar and attention than peaches (page 33). The recipe below will also work by directly substituting blueberries, raspberries, and blackberries. It creates a wonderful filling for pies and cakes or a topping for shortbreads or ice cream.

MAKES 8 PINTS

Get your boiling-water-bath canning equipment ready and have your jars sterilized and ready.

4 quarts fresh strawberries
2 cups sugar
3 tablespoons fresh lemon juice

1. Wash and hull the strawberries. If the berries are small, leave them whole; if they are large, cut in halves or quarters. In a large bowl, combine the strawberries, sugar, and lemon juice. Gently stir to evenly coat the berries. Set the bowl aside for at least 2 hours, or up to overnight (if overnight, put the bowl in the refrigerator), so the sugar and juices mingle and create a syrup.

2. Once a syrup has formed, pour the berry mixture into a large pot over medium to medium-high heat and cook for 3 to 5 minutes, or until the mixture is just hot, with tiny bubbles around the edge of the pan. Don't let it boil, or the berries will overcook.

3. Carefully ladle or pour the hot mixture into hot, sterilized jars, leaving $\frac{1}{2}$" of headspace. Gently tap the jars to make sure all the berries are completely surrounded by liquid and there are no air bubbles. Add more hot berry mixture or juice now, if needed.

4. If there is juice left in the bottom of the pot, go ahead and can it, too! It makes a great syrup for pancakes or flavoring for homemade ice cream.

5. Wipe the rim of each jar carefully with a clean towel to ensure a good seal, and carefully place the lids and rims on.

6. Follow your boiling-water-bath canning process and process for 20 minutes, adjusting for altitude based on the chart on page 24.

basic fruits and vegetables

green beans

This is our first pressure-canning recipe, but don't fret—we're starting easy! Green beans, known as string beans in the South, are a wonderful fresh summer vegetable, but canning them lets you enjoy them all year long. While the canned version lacks the crunch that fresh beans offer, it is delicious and satisfying in its own right. When canning green beans, make sure you use fresh young beans for best results.

MAKES 4 QUARTS

Get your pressure-canning equipment ready and have your jars sterilized and ready.

8 pounds green beans
4 teaspoons kosher salt

1. Wash and rinse the beans very well, trim the tips, and remove the bean "string."

2. Bring a large pot of water to a boil. Add the beans and blanch for 5 minutes.
Note: This step is much easier if you have a blanching basket or bag, as it lets you load in what you are blanching and pull it out all at once.

3. Carefully remove the beans from the boiling water (keep the pot of water boiling) and pack the beans directly into hot, sterilized jars. It works best if you can pack the beans standing upright like matchsticks. Leave 1" of headspace. Add 1 teaspoon of the salt to each quart jar.

4. Carefully ladle or pour boiling water over the beans, leaving 1" of headspace. Gently tap the jars to make sure all the beans are completely surrounded by liquid and there are no air bubbles. Add more boiling water now, if needed.

5. Wipe the rim of each jar carefully with a clean towel to ensure a good seal, and carefully place the lids and rims on.

6. Follow your pressure-canning process and process at 10 pounds of pressure for 25 minutes, adjusting for altitude based on the chart on page 24.

basic fruits and vegetables

tomatoes

I use tomatoes and tomato sauce in so many recipes throughout the year. I'm a tomato snob, though, and cannot bear to eat fresh tomatoes that aren't field-grown heirloom varieties. So for tomato consumption outside of summertime, I depend on what I can put up. There's debate out there about whether tomatoes are acidic enough to can using the boiling-water-bath method, but for our safety, we're canning here with the pressure-canning method. No one wants a side of botulism with their spaghetti. The recipe below uses whole Roma tomatoes, but you can substitute larger tomatoes and cut them up or even use whole cherry tomatoes.

MAKES 4 QUARTS

Get your pressure-canning equipment ready and have your jars sterilized and ready.

12 pounds Roma tomatoes

4 teaspoons kosher salt

1. The first step in canning whole tomatoes is peeling them. (You can always leave the peels on, but I find the finished product is easier to use if you peel before canning.) Fill a large bowl with ice water and set to the side. Bring a large pot of water to a boil. Working in batches, drop the tomatoes into the boiling water a few at a time and blanch for 30 to 60 seconds, or until the skin starts to wrinkle and split. Using a slotted spoon, immediately and carefully move them to the ice water. Let them cool in the water for 1 minute before peeling them with your fingers. Repeat until all the tomatoes are peeled.

2. Pack the peeled tomatoes directly into hot, sterilized jars. Stack them in tightly, pressing down with your fingers as you go. Juice will release from the tomatoes and fill in around them. Fill each jar, leaving 1/2" of headspace. Gently tap the jars to make sure all the tomatoes are completely surrounded by liquid and there are no air bubbles. Add 1 teaspoon of the salt to each jar.

3. Wipe the rim of each jar carefully with a clean towel to ensure a good seal, and carefully place the lids and rims on.

4. Follow your pressure-canning process and process the tomatoes at 10 pounds of pressure for 25 minutes, adjusting for altitude based on the chart on page 24.

Note: There is no added water in this recipe, but when the jars come out of the canner, there will likely be juice at the bottom of the jar and "tomato" at the top. This is normal—it's the juice of the tomato separating from the pulp.

peas and beans

My favorite things to eat are steamy warm bowls of field peas or butterbeans (lima beans to those of you outside the South). They are earthy, delicious, and so good for you. Canning lets you enjoy them longer and is a great way to have a quick meal or dinner side that heats up in just minutes. The recipe below is for butterbeans, but you can use the same technique for any bean (lima beans, navy beans, chickpeas) or field pea (black-eyed peas, crowder peas, red peas).

MAKES 6 PINTS

Get your pressure-canning equipment ready and have your jars sterilized and ready.

12 pounds fresh butterbeans, shelled
6 teaspoons kosher salt

1. Shell and wash the beans thoroughly and discard any bad beans.

2. Fill a large bowl with ice water and set to the side. Bring a large pot of water to a boil. Add the beans, bring the water back to a boil, and blanch for 3 minutes. Immediately use a slotted spoon to carefully move the beans to the ice water. Let them cool in the water for 1 minute.
Note: This step is much easier if you have a blanching basket or bag, as it lets you load in what you are blanching and pull it out all at once.

3. Pack the beans directly into hot, sterilized jars, leaving $1/2$" of headspace. Add 1 teaspoon of the salt to each jar.

4. Meanwhile, bring another pot of water to a boil. Carefully ladle or pour boiling water over the beans, leaving 1" of headspace. Gently tap the jars to make sure all the beans are completely surrounded by liquid and there are no air bubbles.

5. Wipe the rim of each jar carefully with a clean towel to ensure a good seal, and carefully place the lids and rims on.

6. Follow your pressure-canning process and process at 10 pounds of pressure for 40 minutes, adjusting for altitude based on the chart on page 24.

basic fruits and vegetables

corn

Corn is an ingredient in so many recipes. I add it to soups, salads, casseroles, breads, and dips. I hate buying it in metal cans that make it taste horrible. Fresh corn is so easy to can, you won't ever have to buy it at the store again.

MAKES 6 PINTS

Get your pressure-canning equipment ready and have your jars sterilized and ready.

12–18 pounds corn, in the husk

3 teaspoons kosher salt

1. Shuck the corn, clean off all silks, and wash the ears thoroughly. Hold an ear of corn vertically against a cutting board and slice downward to remove the kernels from the cob. Place the kernels in a colander, and repeat with the remaining ears. Rinse thoroughly one more time.

2. Pack the kernels loosely into hot, sterilized jars, leaving $\frac{1}{2}$" of headspace. Add $\frac{1}{2}$ teaspoon of the salt to each jar.

3. Meanwhile, bring a large pot of water to a boil. Carefully ladle or pour boiling water over the corn, leaving 1" of head-space. Gently tap the jars to make sure all the corn is completely surrounded by liquid and there are no air bubbles.

4. Wipe the rim of each jar carefully with a clean towel to ensure a good seal, and carefully place the lids and rims on.

5. Follow your pressure-canning process and process at 10 pounds of pressure for 55 minutes, adjusting for altitude based on the chart on page 24.

new potatoes

Tiny new potatoes are one of my favorite things to can. It's the best way to save that fresh-dug new potato flavor and tenderness. Plus, canned potatoes make the easiest dinnertime side dish. Just open the jar, add a little butter and a handful of herbs, heat them up, and you're ready to go. Small potatoes work best for canning.

MAKES 6 PINTS

Get your pressure-canning equipment ready and have your jars sterilized and ready.

9 pounds new potatoes, such as red or Yukon Gold
3 teaspoons kosher salt

1. Thoroughly wash and peel the potatoes. If they are large, cut into 1" pieces. If small, leave them whole. (They are better when they are small and left whole.)

2. Bring a large pot of water to a boil. Add the potatoes, bring back to a boil, and cook for 2 minutes. Remove the potatoes from the water and pack them directly into hot, sterilized jars, leaving 1" of headspace. Add $1/2$ teaspoon of the salt to each jar.

3. Meanwhile, bring another pot of water to a boil. Carefully ladle or pour boiling water over the potatoes, again leaving 1" of headspace. Gently tap the jars to make sure all the potatoes are completely surrounded by liquid and there are no air bubbles.

4. Wipe the rim of each jar carefully with a clean towel to ensure a good seal, and carefully place the lids and rims on.

5. Follow your pressure-canning process and process at 10 pounds of pressure for 35 minutes, adjusting for altitude based on the chart on page 24.

basic fruits and vegetables

greens

This recipe is included for historic value. Both of my grandmothers canned greens, and so did their mothers. It's what you did before you had big freezers. Nowadays most people preserve greens by freezing, if they preserve them at all, but I think canning captures some of their flavor and makes the end product so much easier to use. This recipe can be used for any leafy green like spinach, kale, chard, or collards and can be seasoned with sprinkles of herbs, garlic, or mustard seeds in each jar. Use fresh-picked leaves. The canned results are great additions to soups, stews, and stuffings. Be warned that blanching greens shrinks them a lot, so it will take a mountain of greens to fill a few pint jars.

MAKES 6 PINTS

Get your pressure-canning equipment ready and have your jars sterilized and ready.

12 pounds leafy greens (kale, chard, spinach, or collards)
3 teaspoons kosher salt

1. Thoroughly wash the greens, then rinse them again. Greens hold on to dirt, so several washing steps are usually necessary. Cut the center stems out and chop the leaves into 1" strips.

2. Fill a large bowl with ice water and set to the side. Bring a large pot of water to a boil. Add the greens, bring back to a boil, and blanch for 1 to 2 minutes, or until the greens start to wilt. Immediately remove the greens and submerge in the ice water. Let them cool in the water for 1 minute.
Note: This step is much easier if you have a blanching basket or bag, as it lets you load in what you are blanching and pull it out all at once.

3. Remove the greens from the ice water, carefully draining away the water, and pack them directly into hot, sterilized jars, leaving 1" of headspace. Add ½ teaspoon of the salt to each jar.

4. Meanwhile, bring another pot of water to a boil. Pour boiling water over the greens, again leaving 1" of headspace. Gently tap the jars to make sure all the greens are completely surrounded by liquid and there are no air bubbles.

5. Wipe the rim of each jar carefully with a clean towel to ensure a good seal, and carefully place the lids and rims on.

6. Follow your pressure-canning process and process the greens at 10 pounds of pressure for 1 hour 10 minutes, adjusting for altitude based on the chart on page 24.

cherry pie

Not that you need ideas for what to do with delicious canned cherries, but this pie is a perfect use for them. It's always a hit at family gatherings and potlucks.

MAKES 1 PIE

2 unbaked piecrusts
2 pints canned cherries
(page 36)
1 cup sugar
3 tablespoons cornstarch
1 tablespoon butter
$\frac{1}{2}$ teaspoon ground cinnamon

1. Preheat the oven to 425°F. Line a 9" pie pan with one piecrust.
2. Drain the cherries over a bowl, reserving the liquid.
3. In a small saucepan over medium heat, combine the sugar, cornstarch, and 1 cup of the reserved cherry liquid. Cook, stirring constantly, for 5 to 10 minutes, or until the mixture starts to bubble. Cook 1 minute longer and remove from the heat.
4. Stir in the butter, cinnamon, and cherries and pour into the prepared crust.
5. Cut the second piecrust into lattice strips and layer the strips in a crosshatch lattice pattern over the top of the pie. Place the pie pan on a large rimmed baking dish in case the juices bubble over.
6. Bake for 10 minutes, then reduce the heat to 350°F and bake for 30 to 35 minutes, or until the crust is golden brown. Let the pie cool and set for at least 15 minutes before serving.

basic fruits and vegetables

succotash

Succotash can be a blend of most any vegetables. Corn with butterbeans is a favorite combination in our house and is a great way to use the corn, butterbeans, or peas you canned.

MAKES 4–6 SERVINGS

1 pint canned corn (page 44), drained

1 pint canned butterbeans (page 43), drained

2 tablespoons olive oil

4 large cloves garlic, finely chopped

2 tablespoons unsalted butter

2 tablespoons fresh basil, roughly chopped

Kosher salt and ground black pepper

1. Open the jars of corn and butterbeans and drain off the canning juice.

2. In a large cast-iron skillet over medium heat, warm the oil. Add the garlic and cook for 1 minute. Add the corn and butterbeans and stir well to coat with the oil. Cover the pan and cook for 5 minutes.

3. Remove the lid and test the beans to see if they are tender. If not, put the lid back on and cook, stirring occasionally, for 5 minutes, or until the butterbeans are tender and the corn starts to brown.

4. Stir in the butter and basil and cook, uncovered, for 5 minutes.

5. Remove from the heat and season to taste with salt and pepper. Serve immediately.

corn pudding

This savory sweet dish is a Southern tradition much loved in my family. It graced the table for every family meal or holiday dinner I can remember. It tastes like the love child of cornbread and rice pudding—a match made in heaven.

MAKES 6–8 SERVINGS

4 tablespoons sugar

3 tablespoons all-purpose flour

2 teaspoons baking powder

1½ teaspoons kosher salt

1 teaspoon ground black pepper

6 large eggs

2 cups heavy cream

½ cup butter, melted and cooled

3 pints canned corn (page 44), drained

1. Preheat the oven to 350°F. Butter a 9" × 13" baking dish.

2. In a medium mixing bowl, combine the sugar, flour, baking powder, salt, and pepper.

3. In a large mixing bowl, whisk together the eggs, cream, and butter. Gradually add the flour mixture in increments, whisking after every addition until incorporated. Add the drained corn and mix well.

4. Transfer to the prepared baking dish and bake for 40 to 45 minutes, or until the top is brown and the center doesn't wiggle when you shake the pan. Let cool for 15 minutes before serving.

basic fruits and vegetables

CHAPTER 2

jams, jellies, preserves, and other sweets

This section is the sweet spot. We're digging deep to cover sweet preparations for canning. These are some of the first recipes I learned to can growing up. My mother loves to make preserves and give them to everyone she knows, so we spent lots of afternoons stirring a giant sugary pot. Your house will smell great, and there won't be a bare piece of toast in your house all year long.

Be forewarned, jam and jelly making can be tricky at the beginning. You will burn batches, and you will end up with a runny mess at times. The vagaries of nature and time that take their toll on fruits and vegetables will be passed on to you. If you are cooking with fruit that was picked when it was wet outside, it will often take much longer to cook down to your desired consistency. If it was picked during a drought, it will cook faster than you can imagine. Be brave! Throw the bad batch out and start again (Actually, never throw out the runny ones. They are almost always delicious on pancakes and waffles.) The more jam and jelly you make, the better you get at reading the process.

Many recipes for jams and jellies rely on pectin and gelatin to thicken and stabilize things, but I don't love the flavor those impart. You don't need the additives for preservation: I just count on the sugar and a little extra canning time to get the job done.

Note: A quick trick that you will use a lot in these recipes is the "cold-plate test." You perform this test by placing a saucer in your freezer when you start to cook. Pull this cold saucer out and drop a teaspoon of your jam or jelly onto the cold plate. Tilt it sideways a bit and watch the mixture. If it runs easily, it needs to cook more. If it basically stays put, the jam is ready.

Truth be told, this chapter could be subtitled "Fun with Citrus," because it also includes marmalades and curds. These are essentially jams and spreads with a citrus base. Marmalades can have a pleasant bitterness to them because you are using the skins from the fruit as well as the flesh. The bitterness is a welcome contrast to the sugar used for preserving. Curds are more creamy and dense, as they have an egg-and-butter base. Both make great additions to any tea tray and are divinely delicious paired with any creamy dessert.

concord grape jam

America's favorite jam! Grape jam and jelly are ubiquitous in kids' lunch boxes and in grocery store aisles. There's a good reason for this. It's simply delicious and a process any home canner should master.

MAKES 6–7 HALF-PINTS

Get your boiling-water-bath canning equipment ready and have your jars sterilized and ready.

5 pounds fresh Concord grapes, stemmed

5 cups sugar, divided

3 tablespoons fresh lemon juice

1. Peel the skins off the grapes by holding each grape between your thumb and forefinger and squeezing to pop the skin off the grape flesh. Place the skins and flesh in separate bowls. This step takes some time—get the kids to help.

2. In a food processor, process the skins and 1 cup of the sugar until a puree forms. In a large heavy pot over medium heat, bring the pureed skins, grape flesh, lemon juice, and the remaining 4 cups sugar to a boil. Keep boiling, stirring frequently and skimming the foam, for about 20 minutes, or until the fruit is broken down.

3. Set a food mill or a strainer over a large bowl. Carefully pour in the grape mixture and force through all the syrupy liquid. Discard the solids and skin pieces. Return the jam to the pot and cook over medium heat to reach a slow boil. Cook, stirring frequently and skimming any foam from the top, for 30 to 35 minutes. Use the cold-plate test (page 55) to determine when the jam has reached the right consistency.

4. When the jam is done, carefully ladle or pour the hot jam into hot, sterilized jars, leaving $1/2$" of headspace.

5. Wipe the rim of each jar carefully with a clean towel to ensure a good seal, and carefully place the lids and rims on.

6. Follow your boiling-water-bath canning process and process for 10 minutes, adjusting for altitude based on the chart on page 24.

jams, jellies, preserves, and other sweets

peach-rosemary jam

Peach jam is one of my favorites. It tastes so perfect paired with salted butter on toast that it's almost a crime to ever do anything else with it. That being said, this jam, especially with the rosemary addition, is so versatile. Aside from being a divine toast companion, it's wonderful in cookies, on roll-ups, and as a dessert topping.

MAKES 6–7 HALF-PINTS

Get your boiling-water-bath canning equipment ready and have your jars sterilized and ready.

4 pounds fresh peaches

2 tablespoons fresh lemon juice

$\frac{1}{2}$ cup water

3 cups sugar

4 sprigs fresh rosemary, washed and patted dry

1. Fill a large bowl with ice water and set to the side. Bring a large pot of water to a boil. Drop the peaches into the boiling water, making sure they are all submerged. (Work in batches, if necessary.) Blanch the peaches for about 3 minutes, or until you can easily peel the skin off a cooled peach by hand. Using a slotted spoon, carefully transfer the peaches to the ice water. Let them cool in the water for 1 minute.

2. Using your fingers, quickly remove the skins from all the peaches. Cut the peaches in half, remove the pits, and cut the halves into $\frac{1}{2}$" chunks. Place in another large bowl. Add the lemon juice and gently stir to evenly coat the peaches (this prevents them from turning brown). If you want really smooth jam, run the mixture through a food processor.

3. In a large pot over medium heat, combine the $\frac{1}{2}$ cup water and sugar, stirring until the sugar is dissolved. Add the peaches and stir to combine. With a large fork, potato masher, or ricer, crush the peaches as you stir. Break up the pieces to your desired consistency. Stir in the rosemary sprigs. (Do not remove the leaves from the stems.)

4. Cook the jam over medium heat, stirring frequently to keep it from burning on the bottom. The cooking time will depend on how much moisture was in the raw peaches: It can take anywhere from 30 minutes to 2 hours. After 30 minutes, use the cold-plate test (page 55) to determine when the jam has reached the right consistency.

5. When the jam is done, use a slotted spoon to remove and discard the rosemary sprigs. Carefully ladle or pour the hot jam into hot, sterilized jars, leaving $\frac{1}{2}$" of headspace.

6. Wipe the rim of each jar carefully with a clean towel to ensure a good seal, and carefully place the lids and rims on.

7. Follow your boiling-water-bath canning process and process for 10 minutes, adjusting for altitude based on the chart on page 24.

strawberry-honey preserves

This is a wonderful twist on traditional strawberry preserves—sweetened with honey instead of sugar. It has a beautiful super-strawberry-y flavor that is delicious as a traditional toast topping but also an appropriate topping for yogurt or granola.

MAKES 7–8 HALF-PINTS

Get your boiling-water-bath canning equipment ready and have your jars sterilized and ready.

6 pounds fresh strawberries

2 small Granny Smith apples, skin on, cored and cut into slices

1½ tablespoons fresh lemon juice

3¾ cups honey

1. Wash and hull the strawberries, then cut each strawberry in half (or quarters if large). Place the berries in a large heavy pot.

2. Finely grate the apples or process the slices in a food processor, then add them to the strawberries. Add the lemon juice and honey and stir well to incorporate.

3. Cook the strawberry mixture over high heat, stirring regularly, until the mixture begins to boil. Immediately reduce the heat to medium-low and simmer for about 15 minutes, or until the strawberries become soft. Use a potato masher or ricer to break up the strawberries some. Alternatively, process with an immersion blender for a smoother finish.

4. Continue to simmer over medium-low heat, stirring regularly to prevent the fruit from sticking to the pan and burning, for 15 to 45 minutes. (Wetter berries take longer to cook down.) The longer the mixture simmers, the thicker the consistency—but be careful, because you don't want the preserves to caramelize. Use the cold-plate test (page 55) to determine when the preserves have reached the right consistency.

5. When the preserves are done, carefully ladle or pour the hot preserves into hot, sterilized jars, leaving ½" of headspace.

6. Wipe the rim of each jar carefully with a clean towel to ensure a good seal, and carefully place the lids and rims on.

7. Follow your boiling-water-bath canning process and process for 10 minutes, adjusting for altitude based on the chart on page 24.

apple jelly

Apple jelly is a sure sign that summer is ending and fall is on the way. You can use most any apple for this recipe, but I like to mix things up a bit to get the best flavor. I mix tart and sweet apples. Be sure to always use the freshest you can get for the best results.

MAKES 6 HALF-PINTS

Get your boiling-water-bath canning equipment ready and have your jars sterilized and ready.

5 pounds apples

6 cups water

3 tablespoons fresh lemon juice

4 cups sugar

1. Wash the apples well and cut them into small pieces, including the skin and cores. If you have a blanching bag or basket, put the apple pieces in it for this step.

2. In a large heavy pot over high heat, bring the apple pieces and the water to a rolling boil, then reduce the heat to low and simmer for 20 minutes, or until the apples are soft.

3. If you used a blanching bag or basket, carefully pull it from the pot and let all the juice drain back into the pot. Otherwise, strain the juice from the apples into a large bowl, then return the juice to the pot. You should have 5 cups of juice—if not, add water to get 5 cups. Discard the apple pulp.

4. Return the pot of apple juice to high heat, stir in the lemon juice and sugar, and bring to a rolling boil. Continue to boil over high heat, stirring often and skimming off and discarding any foam, until the jelly sets. Cooking time varies greatly based on the pectin level in the apples used: Start testing after 20 minutes. Use the cold-plate test (page 55) to determine when the jelly has reached the right consistency.

5. When the jelly is done, carefully ladle or pour the hot jelly into hot, sterilized jars, leaving $\frac{1}{4}$" of headspace.

6. Wipe the rim of each jar carefully with a clean towel to ensure a good seal, and carefully place the lids and rims on.

7. Follow your boiling-water-bath canning process and process for 5 minutes, adjusting for altitude based on the chart on page 24.

blackberry jam

This traditional jam recipe is very versatile. You can use blackberries as I do here or substitute most any berry, including strawberries, blueberries, raspberries, currants, or lingonberries. This version is rustic and makes a chunky jam with whole berries, but you can always add a step and process the jam through a food mill or with an immersion blender for a finer finish.

MAKES 6–7 HALF-PINTS

Get your boiling-water-bath canning equipment ready and have your jars sterilized and ready.

10 cups fresh blackberries
5 cups sugar
2 tablespoons fresh lemon juice
1 tablespoon lemon zest

1. In a large heavy pot over medium heat, stir together the berries, sugar, lemon juice, and lemon zest and cook, stirring frequently, until the sugar dissolves. Increase the heat to medium–high and bring everything to a boil, still stirring regularly.

2. When the berries have softened, use a potato masher or ricer to press the berries just enough to break them down and release some of their juices. You can keep the texture chunky with almost whole fruit or break things down further. Continue to simmer the mixture over medium heat for 15 to 45 minutes, stirring frequently to prevent the jam from sticking to the pan and burning, and skimming and discarding the foam from the surface as you go. (Wetter berries take longer to cook down.) The longer the mixture simmers, the thicker the consistency—but be careful, because you don't want the jam to caramelize. Use the cold–plate test (page 55) to determine when the jam has reached the right consistency.

3. When the jam is done, very carefully ladle or pour the hot jam into hot, sterilized jars, leaving 1/2" of headspace.

4. Wipe the rim of each jar carefully with a clean towel to ensure a good seal, and carefully place the lids and rims on.

5. Follow your boiling-water-bath canning process and process for 15 minutes, adjusting for altitude based on the chart on page 24.

pear preserves

This recipe is one made in rural kitchens across North Carolina. Simple and delicious, with pure pear flavor, it is wonderful on plain toast but a decadent delight on crostini with goat cheese or poured over a baked brie.

MAKES 6 HALF-PINTS

Get your boiling-water-bath canning equipment ready and have your jars sterilized and ready.

6 pounds fresh pears
1 cinnamon stick
2 teaspoons whole cloves
2 tablespoons fresh lemon juice
4 cups sugar

1. Wash and peel the pears, then core them and cut into small pieces. Put the cinnamon stick and cloves into an herb bag and tie it well.

2. In a large heavy pot over medium heat, combine the pears, herb bag, lemon juice, and sugar and cook, stirring frequently to prevent sticking, for 2 to 2$\frac{1}{2}$ hours. Skim off and discard any foam from the top as you go.

3. When the preserves are as thick as you want them, remove and discard the herb bag. Carefully ladle or pour the hot preserves into hot, sterilized jars, leaving $\frac{1}{4}$" of headspace.

4. Wipe the rim of each jar carefully with a clean towel to ensure a good seal, and carefully place the lids and rims on.

5. Follow your boiling-water-bath canning process and process for 10 minutes, adjusting for altitude based on the chart on page 24.

jams, jellies, preserves, and other sweets

whole fig preserves

This is another traditional recipe that can take on new life on a gourmet table. I grew up eating these on cheese biscuits, but they also make a beautiful appetizer paired with endive and fresh goat cheese. Brown Turkey figs are the variety most available, but this recipe will work with any variety—Black Mission figs make an especially rich version.

MAKES 4 PINTS

Get your boiling-water-bath canning equipment ready and have your jars sterilized and ready.

5 pounds fresh figs, stemmed
3 cups water
1 cup honey
$\frac{1}{2}$ cup sugar
4 tablespoons fresh lemon juice

1. Wash the figs well and place them in a large heavy pot. Cover them with 2" of water and bring to a boil. Reduce the heat to medium low and simmer for 2 minutes. Drain the water and transfer the figs to a large bowl.

2. In the same large pot over high heat, bring the 3 cups water, honey, sugar, and lemon juice to a boil. Stir to dissolve the sugar and keep it from sticking. Add the figs, reduce the heat to medium, and gently boil for 5 to 10 minutes, or until the syrup starts to thicken.

3. Use a slotted spoon to carefully transfer the figs from the syrup pot to hot, sterilized jars. Evenly distribute the figs among the jars, packing them in gently but firmly.

4. When all the figs have been distributed, carefully ladle or pour the hot syrup over the figs to completely cover them. Leave $\frac{1}{2}$" of headspace. Screw the lids on the jars temporarily. Gently swirl each jar to release trapped air bubbles. Remove the lids and add syrup, if necessary, to achieve the proper headspace.

5. Wipe the rim of each jar carefully with a clean towel to ensure a good seal, and carefully place the lids and rims on.

6. Follow your boiling-water-bath canning process and process for 10 minutes, adjusting for altitude based on the chart on page 24.

jams, jellies, preserves, and other sweets

tart cherry preserves

This recipe is designed for the small, tart pie cherries I grew up with in the South. It can be adapted for Bing cherries as well: Just reduce the sugar by a cup or half cup, depending on how sweet you like it.

MAKES 6 HALF-PINTS

Get your boiling-water-bath canning equipment ready and have your jars sterilized and ready.

6 cups fresh sweet cherries
$\frac{1}{2}$ cup water
4 cups sugar
4 tablespoons fresh lemon juice

1. Stem, wash, and pit the cherries. The pitting is the hardest part. Put on some good music and settle in. Roughly chop the cherries.
2. In a large heavy pot over medium-high heat, bring the cherries and water to a low boil. Immediately reduce the heat to low and simmer, stirring frequently to prevent sticking, for 15 minutes, or until the cherries begin to break down and thicken.
3. Stir in the sugar and lemon juice. Increase the heat to high to bring everything to a full rolling boil, stirring constantly to prevent sticking. Keep boiling and stirring for about 10 minutes, or until the preserves thicken as much as you want. Use the cold-plate test (page 55) to determine when the preserves have reached the right consistency.

4. When the preserves are done, carefully ladle or pour them into hot, sterilized jars, leaving $\frac{1}{4}$" of headspace.
5. Wipe the rim of each jar carefully with a clean towel to ensure a good seal, and carefully place the lids and rims on.
6. Follow your boiling-water-bath canning process and process for 15 minutes, adjusting for altitude based on the chart on page 24.

blueberry-basil balsamic jam

We're stepping up our game with this jam. The basil and balsamic vinegar add a fun punch to a traditional recipe. This works well in jam's normal format but is also wonderful as a marinade for a slow-cooker pork roast or as a topping on a chicken sandwich. You can directly substitute strawberries, raspberries, or blackberries for the blueberries here.

MAKES 6 HALF-PINTS

Get your boiling-water-bath canning equipment ready and have your jars sterilized and ready.

3 pounds fresh blueberries
$\frac{1}{4}$ cup fresh basil leaves
3 cups sugar
3 tablespoons balsamic vinegar

1. Wash and dry the blueberries and basil. Chop the basil into tiny slivers.

2. In a large, heavy pot, combine the berries and basil and use a potato masher or ricer to roughly break up the berries. Stir in the sugar and let the berries rest in it for about 20 minutes, or until they release some of their juices.

3. When the sugar around the blueberries looks juicy, bring the pot to a boil over medium-high heat. Stir in the vinegar, reduce the heat to medium for a low boil, and cook, stirring regularly, for 15 to 30 minutes, or until the berries soften and the mixture begins to thicken. Use the cold-plate test (page 55) to determine when the jam has reached the right consistency.

4. When the jam is done, carefully ladle or pour the hot jam into hot, sterilized jars, leaving $\frac{1}{4}$" of headspace.

5. Wipe the rim of each jar carefully with a clean towel to ensure a good seal, and carefully place the lids and rims on.

6. Follow your boiling-water-bath canning process and process for 10 minutes, adjusting for altitude based on the chart on page 24.

tomato jam

Think ketchup but more funky. This jam is great on meat and cheese plates, smeared on sandwiches, or to dress up seared chicken breasts.

MAKES 6 HALF-PINTS

Get your boiling-water-bath canning equipment ready and have your jars sterilized and ready.

5 pounds tomatoes, cored and finely chopped

3½ cups sugar

½ cup fresh lime juice

2 teaspoons finely grated fresh ginger

1 teaspoon ground cinnamon

2 cloves garlic, minced

1 tablespoon sea salt

½ tablespoon red-pepper flakes

1. In a large heavy pot over high heat, combine the tomatoes, sugar, lime juice, ginger, cinnamon, garlic, salt, and pepper flakes. Use a potato masher or ricer to break down the tomatoes a little. Bring to a boil, then reduce the heat to low and simmer, stirring regularly, for 1½ to 2 hours, or until the mixture starts to thicken and get sticky.

2. Be very careful about stirring—the tomatoes will begin to stick badly as they get more done and will burn on the bottom of the pot if you are not vigilant. Keep stirring frequently all along, but check more closely after 1¼ hours. Use the cold-plate test (page 55) to determine when the jam has reached the right consistency.

3. When the jam is done, carefully ladle or pour the hot jam into hot, sterilized jars, leaving ½" of headspace.

4. Wipe the rim of each jar carefully with a clean towel to ensure a good seal, and carefully place the lids and rims on.

5. Follow your boiling-water-bath canning process and process for 15 minutes, adjusting for altitude based on the chart on page 24.

pepper jelly

In the South, this jelly is all over every family reunion spread on top of cream cheese and served with crackers. Sounds a little iffy, but don't knock it 'til you try it. You'll love it. You'll love it even more on grilled cheese sandwiches or open-faced turkey melts.

MAKES 6 HALF-PINTS

Get your boiling-water-bath canning equipment ready and have your jars sterilized and ready.

4 pounds tart apples
6 jalapeño chile peppers, wear plastic gloves when handling
1 red bell pepper
3 cups water
3 cups white vinegar
3½ cups sugar

1. Wash and dry the apples and peppers. Cut the apples, including the cores, into small pieces. Wearing gloves, cut the jalapeños lengthwise. For a hot jelly, keep all the seeds. If you want a milder jelly, discard half of the seeds. Cut the bell pepper into strips and discard the seeds and ribs.

2. In a large pot over high heat, bring the apple pieces, jalapeños, bell pepper, water, and vinegar to a boil. Immediately reduce the heat to medium-low and simmer for about 20 minutes, or until the apples and peppers are soft. Stir frequently to prevent sticking.

3. When the apples are good and soft, use a potato masher or ricer to mash the apples until they feel like baby applesauce. Carefully pour the contents of the pot into a mesh or cheesecloth-lined sieve set over a large bowl and let the liquid strain out for at least 2 hours. Don't force things: Let gravity pull the juices out for the best results.

4. Measure the juice (you should have 4 cups) and pour it into a large heavy pot. Add the sugar at a ratio of 3½ cups of sugar to 4 cups of juice. Stir the sugar in well. Heat over medium-high heat to bring to a boil, then lower the heat to medium and cook at a low boil, stirring regularly, for 10 to 15 minutes. Skim off and discard any foam. Use the cold-plate test (page 55) to determine when the jelly has reached the right consistency.

5. When the jelly is done, carefully ladle or pour the hot jelly into hot, sterilized jars, leaving ¼" of headspace.

6. Wipe the rim of each jar carefully with a clean towel to ensure a good seal, and carefully place the lids and rims on.

7. Follow your boiling-water-bath canning process and process for 10 minutes, adjusting for altitude based on the chart on page 24.

onion jam

This savory sweet jam is great to keep in the pantry all the time. It dresses up a meat and cheese platter beautifully, adds a burst of flavor to goat cheese crostini, and serves as a magical secret ingredient for sandwiches and stuffings.

MAKES 4 HALF-PINTS

Get your boiling-water-bath canning equipment ready and have your jars sterilized and ready.

1/4 cup olive oil

2 pounds sweet onions, diced

1 pound shallots, diced

1/2 cup firmly packed light brown sugar

2 cups dry red wine

6 tablespoons balsamic vinegar

1 tablespoon dried rosemary

1/2 teaspoon kosher salt

1/2 tablespoon ground black pepper

1. In a heavy pot over medium heat, add the oil and stir together the onions and shallots. Cook until the onions soften, then add the sugar and cook uncovered, stirring regularly to prevent sticking, for 45 to 60 minutes, or until the onions and shallots start to brown and all the liquid has evaporated.

2. Add the wine, vinegar, rosemary, salt, and pepper and bring to a boil over medium-high heat. Reduce the heat to low and simmer for 45 to 60 minutes, or until the liquid has reduced and the mixture has thickened. Keep stirring frequently. Use the cold-plate test (page 55) to determine when the jam has reached the right consistency.

3. When the jam is done, very carefully ladle or pour the hot jam into hot, sterilized jars, leaving 1/2" of headspace.

4. Wipe the rim of each jar carefully with a clean towel to ensure a good seal, and carefully place the lids and rims on.

5. Follow your boiling-water-bath canning process and process for 10 minutes, adjusting for altitude based on the chart on page 24.

grapefruit marmalade

I grew up a grapefruit hater with two parents who adored them. They could eat grapefruits all day every day. This recipe taught me how to tolerate the flavor of grapefruit. The sweetness of the marmalade provides a welcome foil to grapefruit's natural bitterness. This recipe can be used with any citrus: Just directly substitute fruit by weight.

MAKES 6 HALF-PINTS

Get your boiling-water-bath canning equipment ready and have your jars sterilized and ready.

5 pounds ripe grapefruits (use pink grapefruits, if available)

6 cups sugar

4 cups water

1. Wash and dry the grapefruits well. Using a very sharp peeler or small paring knife, remove the peel from the outside of the fruit. Remove only the colored part of the citrus skin—discard the white pith underneath, as it is bitter. Once you have all the peel off the grapefruits, roughly chop it into chunky 1/2" pieces and set it aside.

2. Carefully open each individual section of grapefruit over a bowl to catch the juices, then separate the actual fruit segments from the membranes. Put the fruit pieces in the bowl with the juice. Pick out the seeds and set them aside. Squeeze any remaining juice out of the membranes into the bowl and put the membranes with the seeds.

3. Place the seeds and membranes into an herb bag or piece of cheesecloth, and tie it well. These will provide natural pectin to help the marmalade set properly.

4. In a large heavy pot over high heat, combine the peel, fruit, juice, sugar, water, and herb/pectin bag. Bring to a boil, stirring often to prevent sticking. Once the mixture is at a good rolling boil, let it cook for

5 minutes, still stirring often. Use the cold-plate test (page 55) to determine when the marmalade has reached the right consistency. If it hasn't, reduce to medium and cook until the right consistency is reached.

5. When the marmalade is done, remove the herb/pectin bag from the pot and carefully ladle or pour the hot marmalade into hot, sterilized jars, leaving 1/2" of headspace.

6. Wipe the rim of each jar carefully with a clean towel to ensure a good seal, and carefully place the lids and rims on.

7. Follow your boiling-water-bath canning process and process for 10 minutes, adjusting for altitude based on the chart on page 24.

lemon curd

I can eat lemon curd with a spoon, directly out of the jar. No toast needed. It's like a spoonable version of a lemon bar. It's good by itself, spread on a scone, as a cake or tart filler, or as an ice cream topping. The recipe below isn't as eggy as some, and that makes it more approachable for new converts. If you are lucky enough to have access to the sweeter Meyer lemons, use them! The end result is even better!

MAKES 6 HALF-PINTS

Get your boiling-water-bath canning equipment ready and have your jars sterilized and ready.

6 large lemons
3 cups sugar
1 cup (2 sticks) unsalted butter, at room temperature
8 extra-large eggs
1 cup fresh lemon juice
$\frac{1}{4}$ teaspoon kosher salt

1. Wash and dry the lemons well. Using a very sharp peeler or small paring knife, remove the peel from the outside of the fruit. Remove only the colored part of the citrus skin—discard the white pith underneath, as it is very bitter.
2. In a food processor, pulse the peel and sugar until the peel is finely minced and mixed with the sugar.
3. In a large bowl, and with an electric mixer on medium speed, cream the butter. Add the lemon mixture and beat on medium for 2 to 3 minutes, or until well mixed and smooth. Keep the mixer going and add the eggs one at a time, beating well after each addition. Then add the lemon juice and salt. Mix for about 2 minutes, or until everything is combined and smooth.
4. Pour 2" of water into the bottom pan of a double boiler and heat until the water boils gently. Pour the curd mixture into the top pan, set it over the boiling water, reduce the heat to low, and cook, stirring constantly to prevent sticking and burning, for about 10 minutes, or until the mixture reaches 170°F on a thermometer and starts to thicken. As you stir, you will feel the curd begin to thicken just before the pot starts to simmer at 170°F. Watch the edges of the pot for bubbles. If you see them, remove it from the heat immediately and check the temperature. Stop cooking when the curd reaches 170°F. If the curd isn't as thick as you want it, keep stirring after you take it off the heat for a couple of minutes and it will thicken.
5. When the curd is done, carefully ladle or pour the hot curd into hot, sterilized jars, leaving $\frac{1}{2}$" of headspace.
6. Wipe the rim of each jar carefully with a clean towel to ensure a good seal, and carefully place the lids and rims on.
7. Follow your boiling-water-bath canning process and process for 15 minutes, adjusting for altitude based on the chart on page 24.

orange-ginger marmalade

This recipe is plain orange marmalade's sexy cousin. The ginger gives it a nice spicy kick. In winter, I stir a teaspoon of it into my hot tea for a soothing treat!

MAKES 6 HALF-PINTS

Get your boiling-water-bath canning equipment ready and have your jars sterilized and ready.

5 pounds ripe sweet oranges, such as Valencia

¼ cup grated fresh ginger

6 cups sugar

4 cups water

1. Wash and dry the oranges well. Using a very sharp peeler or small paring knife, remove the peel from the outside of the fruit. Remove only the colored part of the citrus skin—discard the white pith underneath, as it is very bitter. Once you have all the peel off the oranges, roughly chop it into chunky ½" pieces and set it aside.

2. Carefully open each individual orange section over a bowl to catch the juices, then separate the actual fruit segments from the membranes. Put the fruit pieces in the bowl with the juice. Pick out the seeds and set them aside. Squeeze any remaining juice out of the membranes into the bowl and put them with the seeds.

3. Place the seeds and membranes into an herb bag or a piece of cheesecloth, and tie it well. These will provide natural pectin to help the marmalade set properly.

4. In a large heavy pot over high heat, combine the peel, fruit, juice, ginger, sugar, water, and herb/pectin bag. Bring to a boil, stirring often to prevent sticking. Once the mixture is at a good rolling boil, let it cook for 5 minutes, still stirring often. Use the cold-plate test (page 55) to determine when the marmalade has reached the right consistency. If it hasn't, reduce heat to medium and cook until right consistency is reached.

5. When marmalade is done, remove the herb/pectin bag from the pot and carefully ladle or pour the hot marmalade into hot, sterilized jars, leaving ½" of headspace.

6. Wipe the rim of each jar carefully with a clean towel to ensure a good seal, and carefully place the lids and rims on.

7. Follow your boiling-water-bath canning process and process for 10 minutes, adjusting for altitude based on the chart on page 24.

cranberry-orange curd

Hello, holidays! This recipe is perfect to have around during the fall and winter season. It makes a great addition for family breakfasts and is a beautiful option for hostess gifts—the finished product is a creamy burgundy. It's also a wonderful topping for a cream cheese tart!

MAKES 4 HALF-PINTS

Get your boiling-water-bath canning equipment ready and have your jars sterilized and ready.

24 ounces fresh cranberries (usually 2 bags)

1 cup water

¼ cup fresh orange juice

1½ tablespoons finely grated orange peel (from 1 orange)

1 cup granulated sugar

½ cup firmly packed light brown sugar

4 tablespoons unsalted butter, at room temperature

2 eggs

4 egg yolks

1½ teaspoons cornstarch

½ teaspoon ground cinnamon

¼ teaspoon kosher salt

1. In a medium heavy pot over high heat, bring the cranberries, water, orange juice, and orange peel to a rolling boil. Reduce the heat to low and simmer for 10 minutes, or until the cranberries start to soften. Stir as the water cooks down to prevent sticking.

2. Pour the cranberry mixture into a blender or food processor and process until smooth. If you have used a high-powered blender (such as a Vitamix), move on to the next step. If not, strain the mixture through a fine sieve or food mill set over a bowl, so that you have a smooth finish. Set aside to cool.

3. In a large bowl, and with an electric mixer on medium speed, cream the granulated sugar, brown sugar, and butter for 3 minutes, or until well mixed and smooth. Keep the mixer running on medium and add the eggs and yolks one at a time, beating well after each addition. Then add the cornstarch, cinnamon, and salt. Mix for about 2 minutes, or until everything is combined and smooth.

4. With the mixer on low speed, slowly pour in the cranberry mixture.

5. Pour 2" of water into the bottom pan of a double boiler and heat until the water boils gently. Pour the curd mixture into the top pan, set it over the boiling water, reduce the heat to low, and cook, stirring constantly to prevent sticking and burning, for 5 to 10 minutes, or until the mixture reaches 170°F on a thermometer and starts to thicken. As you stir, you will feel the curd begin to thicken just before the pot starts to simmer at 170°F. Watch the edges of the pot for bubbles. If you see them, remove it from the heat immediately and check the temperature. Stop cooking when you reach 170°F. If the curd isn't as thick as you want it, keep stirring after you take it off the heat for a couple of minutes and it will thicken.

6. When curd is done, carefully ladle or pour the hot curd into hot, sterilized jars, leaving $\frac{1}{2}$" of headspace.

7. Wipe the rim of each jar carefully with a clean towel to ensure a good seal, and carefully place the lids and rims on.

8. Follow your boiling-water-bath canning process and process for 15 minutes, adjusting for altitude based on the chart on page 24.

jelly roll

Having lots of varieties of jams and jellies on hand makes this simple dessert easy and varied. You can pick a favorite or try something new every time.

MAKES 6–8 SERVINGS

3 eggs
1 cup granulated sugar
$\frac{1}{3}$ cup cold water
2 teaspoons vanilla extract
1 cup all-purpose flour
1 teaspoon cream of tartar
$\frac{1}{2}$ teaspoon baking soda
$\frac{1}{2}$ teaspoon ground cinnamon
2 half-pints Peach–Rosemary
    Jam (page 58), Apple Jelly
    (page 62), Lemon Curd
    (page 77), or Cranberry-
    Orange Curd (page 80)
Confectioner's sugar, for
    garnish
Whipped cream or ice cream,
    for serving

1. Preheat the oven to 375°F. Lightly grease a baking sheet or jelly-roll pan and line with waxed paper or parchment paper. Grease the paper as well.
2. In a large mixing bowl, whisk together the eggs, granulated sugar, water, and vanilla until frothy. Add the flour, cream of tartar, baking soda, and cinnamon and whisk well to incorporate.
3. Pour the batter into a thin layer on the prepared baking sheet. Bake for 8 to 12 minutes, or until the cake is golden brown and springy to the touch.

4. Take a thin kitchen or flour-sack towel and wet it well. Wring it out and spread it on the counter. Invert the cake pan carefully onto the cloth. Carefully pull off the waxed paper and discard. With a smooth spatula, spread the jam or jelly evenly over the cake.
5. Use the edges of the cloth to help you start to tightly roll the cake—like rolling up a poster. When the cake is tightly rolled, place it on a platter, exposed seam down, and dust with confectioner's sugar.
6. To serve, cut the roll into disks and accompany with whipped cream or ice cream.

baked brie with pear preserves

Parties have just gotten much easier at your house: Take a few minutes to heat up the brie, open a jar, and you have a gourmet appetizer.

MAKES 6–8 SERVINGS

1 wheel brie cheese
1 half-pint Pear Preserves (page 65), at room temperature
Salty crackers or baguette, for serving

1. Preheat the oven to 350°F. Line a sheet pan with parchment paper.

2. Place the brie on the prepared pan and bake for 5 to 7 minutes, or until you just start to see the cheese ooze. You do not want it to melt all the way.

3. Transfer the brie to your serving plate. Open the jar of preserves and pour over the hot brie. Put your platter out for snacking and serve with the crackers or the baguette torn into pieces.

endive
fig boats

This recipe is a super no-bake appetizer that works well for crowds, large and small. It's stable at room temperature so can be made ahead of time and set out ready for guests to arrive.

MAKES 10 SMALL SERVINGS

2 endive heads, leaves separated
    and rinsed
½ pound fresh goat cheese
2 pints Whole Fig Preserves
    (page 67)

1. Place the endive leaves on a serving platter in an attractive pattern.
2. Using a small spoon, scoop out the cheese in 1-tablespoon-size portions and place a scoop in each endive leaf.
3. Open the jars of figs and drain the juices into a bowl. (Reserve the juices to serve with a cheese platter.) Place one drained fig on top of the cheese in each endive leaf. If the figs are too big, or you need to make them go further, slice them in half before placing them in the leaves.
4. Clean up any fig juice dribbles and put your platter out for snacking.

CHAPTER 3

pickles

Pickles are a lot easier to make than most people think. In general, they are just cut-up vegetables or fruit preserved in a brine. For shelf-stable canning, we will be pickling in mostly vinegar-based brines.

You'll get the hang of preparing a brine and filling jars, and you'll have an awesome snack when you're done. Make enough to share, and your neighbors will love you.

When canning pickles, you might have extra brine or extra produce when you are done with the recipe. That's okay. It's hard to estimate exact size and liquid content when dealing with fresh produce, so don't worry if you have a little extra. Throw the extras in a salad for dinner.

Pickling spice is an ingredient used in several recipes. It's a blend of many spices, including coriander, allspice, ginger, bay, cinnamon, and pepper. You can make your own or buy it premade in the spice section at most grocery stores. Also, remember that pickles need to sit for a few days after canning before you open the jar and taste them. I try to wait at least a week before cracking open a jar.

cucumber dill pickles

I know I'm not supposed to claim favorites, so don't tell the others . . . but these are my favorite pickles. I eat at least a jar every week, and I have been known to take a big drink of the brine after a long, hot run. They are refreshing and wonderful. Eat them alone as a snack or chop them and use as relish in chicken or egg salad.

MAKES 4 PINTS

Get your boiling-water-bath canning equipment ready and have your jars sterilized and ready.

3 pounds small pickling cucumbers

½ cup kosher salt, plus 3 tablespoons, divided

2 garlic heads, cloves peeled and smashed

4 teaspoons dill seeds

2 teaspoons dill fronds

1 teaspoon mustard seeds

2 cups white vinegar

2 cups water

1. Wash and dry the cucumbers. Cut away the ends and slice the cukes into lengthwise quarters. Place the slices in a large bowl, sprinkle with the ½ cup salt, and cover with 2" of ice. Refrigerate for 3 to 4 hours. Add more ice if needed and drain away the accumulated water when you do. When the chilling period is complete, drain away the water and rinse the slices well.

2. Divide the garlic, dill seeds, dill fronds, and mustard seeds evenly among the hot, sterilized jars. Divide the cucumber spears evenly and pack them into the jars as tightly as you can.

3. To make the brine, in a large stainless steel pot over high heat, bring the vinegar, water, and the remaining 3 tablespoons salt to a rolling boil. Once it boils, remove the pan from the heat and immediately ladle or pour the brine into the jars to cover the cucumbers completely, leaving ¼" of headspace. Gently tap the jars to remove air bubbles.

4. Wipe the rim of each jar carefully with a clean towel to ensure a good seal, and carefully place the lids and rims on.

5. Follow your boiling-water-bath canning process and process for 10 minutes, adjusting for altitude based on the chart on page 24.

sweet cucumber pickles

Pickles are a battleground in my family. I like savory dill pickles. So does my mama. We are the ones on the side of justice. We are the ones who make the pickles. However, everyone we love prefers sweet pickles. So we make batches of both. That also means we make 2 batches of anything that contains pickle relish—from deviled eggs to chicken salad. There's room for all types at our table. We don't judge—until you get up for seconds.

MAKES 8 PINTS

Get your boiling-water-bath canning equipment ready and have your jars sterilized and ready.

8 pounds small pickling cucumbers

$^1/_2$ cup kosher salt

$4^1/_2$ cups sugar

$3^1/_2$ cups apple cider vinegar

2 cups water

2 tablespoons mustard seeds

1 tablespoon ground allspice

1. Wash and dry the cucumbers. Cut away the ends and slice the cukes into $^1/_8$" disks. Place the slices in a large bowl, sprinkle with the salt, and cover with 2" of ice. Refrigerate for 3 to 4 hours. Add more ice if needed and drain away the accumulated water when you do. When the chilling period is complete, drain away the water and rinse the slices well.

2. Divide the cucumber slices evenly among the hot, sterilized jars and pack them into the jars as tightly as you can.

3. To make the brine, in a large stainless steel pot over high heat, bring the sugar, vinegar, water, mustard seeds, and allspice to a rolling boil. Stir occasionally to make sure the sugar isn't sticking. Once it boils, remove the pan from the heat and immediately pour the brine into the jars to cover the cucumbers completely, leaving $^1/_2$" of headspace. Gently tap the jars to remove air bubbles.

4. Wipe the rim of each jar carefully with a clean towel to ensure a good seal, and carefully place the lids and rims on.

5. Follow your boiling-water-bath canning process and process for 10 minutes, adjusting for altitude based on the chart on page 24.

bread-and-butter pickles

These were my daddy's, and his daddy's, favorite pickles. My daddy ate them with a fork straight from the jar and on every sandwich he ever made. They also chop into a lovely relish and pair well with a meat and cheese plate.

MAKES 8 PINTS

Get your boiling-water-bath canning equipment ready and have your jars sterilized and ready.

5 pounds small pickling cucumbers

2 pounds sweet onions, thinly sliced

$\frac{1}{2}$ cup kosher salt

$3\frac{1}{2}$ cups apple cider vinegar

4 cups sugar

10 cloves garlic

2 tablespoons mustard seeds

$1\frac{1}{2}$ teaspoons celery seeds

1 teaspoon red-pepper flakes

$\frac{1}{8}$ teaspoon ground cloves

1 teaspoon ground turmeric

1. Wash and dry the cucumbers. Cut away the ends and slice the cukes into $\frac{1}{8}$" disks. In a large bowl, combine the cucumbers with the onions, sprinkle them with the salt, and cover with 2" of ice. Refrigerate for 3 to 4 hours. Add more ice if needed and drain away the accumulated water when you do. When the chilling period is complete, drain away the water and rinse the slices well.

2. In a large stainless steel pot over high heat, bring the vinegar, sugar, garlic, mustard seeds, celery seeds, pepper flakes, cloves, and turmeric to a rolling boil. Add the cucumbers and onions, stir really well, and bring back to a boil. Remove the pot from the heat.

3. Carefully use tongs or a slotted spoon to evenly divide the cucumbers and onions among the jars, packing them into the jars as tightly as you can. Then fill each jar with brine liquid from the pot to cover the cucumbers and onions completely, leaving $\frac{1}{2}$" of headspace. Gently tap the jars to remove air bubbles.

4. Wipe the rim of each jar carefully with a clean towel to ensure a good seal, and carefully place the lids and rims on.

5. Follow your boiling-water-bath canning process and process for 10 minutes, adjusting for altitude based on the chart on page 24.

zucchini pickles

A pickler can't live on cucumbers alone. You have to shake things up a bit. This recipe is fun because the zucchini look like cucumber pickles, but you get a whole different taste and texture. I like to serve them side by side with dill pickles for a fun contrast.

MAKES 4 PINTS

Get your boiling-water-bath canning equipment ready and have your jars sterilized and ready.

10 small zucchini

3 large sweet onions, sliced into rings

1 cup kosher salt, or more as needed

3 cups sugar

2 cups white wine vinegar

$1\frac{1}{2}$ tablespoons pickling spice

1. Wash and dry the zucchini. Cut away the ends and slice into $\frac{1}{4}$" disks.
2. Spread the sliced zucchini and onions on a sheet pan and sprinkle each layer generously with the salt. Let sit for 1 hour, then rinse off the salt and drain well.
3. Evenly divide the zucchini and onion slices among the jars. Pack them well, but not so tightly that the brine you'll be adding can't move around.
4. To make the brine, in a large stainless steel pot over high heat, bring the sugar, vinegar, and pickling spice to a rolling boil. Remove the pot from the heat and carefully ladle or pour the brine to cover the zucchini and onions completely, leaving $\frac{1}{2}$" of headspace. Gently tap the jars to remove air bubbles.
5. Wipe the rim of each jar carefully with a clean towel to ensure a good seal, and carefully place the lids and rims on.
6. Follow your boiling-water-bath canning process and process for 10 minutes, adjusting for altitude based on the chart on page 24.

watermelon rind pickles

We have stepped up to advanced pickle making with these old-time Southern pickles. They are not actually much harder to make than any other pickle. They just take a little extra time because the rinds need to soak overnight. The flavor is worth the wait, though! The pickle itself is delicious, and the juice makes a wonderful addition to rum cocktails.

MAKES 4 PINTS

Get your boiling-water-bath canning equipment ready and have your jars sterilized and ready.

2 medium watermelons

1 cup kosher salt

8 cups cold water, divided

6 cups sugar

4 cups white wine vinegar

3 cinnamon sticks, broken in half

1 cup crystallized ginger

$\frac{1}{2}$ teaspoon ground allspice

$\frac{1}{2}$ teaspoon ground cloves

1. Cut open the watermelons. Cut out the juicy red part (and save for eating later). Remove the outside peel from the rind and discard the peel. Cut the rind into 1" cubes.

2. In a large glass or stainless steel bowl, layer the rind cubes and sprinkle each layer with salt as you go. Add a few handfuls of ice cubes and 4 cups of the water to cover the cubes, then place a big dinner plate upside down over the cubes. Weigh the plate down with something sturdy. Cover and refrigerate overnight.

3. The next day, drain and rinse the rind in cool water 3 times. Drain well after the final rinse.

4. In a large stainless steel pot over high heat, bring the rind and the remaining 4 cups water to a rolling boil. Reduce the heat to low and simmer for 10 to 15 minutes, depending on the melon, until the rind is fork-tender. Drain the liquid away and set the rind aside to cool.

5. In another large stainless steel pot over high heat, bring the sugar, vinegar, cinnamon, ginger, allspice, and cloves to a boil, stirring occasionally so the sugar doesn't stick on the bottom. Reduce the heat to low and simmer for 3 to 5 minutes, until the sugar is dissolved. Add the rind to the pot and bring back to a boil. Reduce to a simmer again and cook for 1 hour, stirring occasionally, until the rind is translucent.

6. Carefully use a slotted spoon to transfer and evenly distribute the hot rind among the hot, sterilized jars. Discard the cinnamon sticks and carefully ladle or pour the pickling juices to cover the rind completely, leaving $\frac{1}{2}$" of headspace. Gently tap the jars to remove air bubbles.

7. Wipe the rim of each jar carefully with a clean towel to ensure a good seal, and carefully place the lids and rims on.

8. Follow your boiling-water-bath canning process and process for 10 minutes, adjusting for altitude based on the chart on page 24.

sauerkraut

Yes, sauerkraut is technically a pickle. It's a fermented pickle. That's where things get tricky. This is a pretty simple process, but make sure to be extra careful and clean at each step. Any dirt or bacteria that is introduced can mess with the fermentation process and will generate rot instead of delicious kraut. You can use any cabbage you like, but I tend to use red cabbage, as the kraut turns a gorgeous fuchsia color that brightens any dish. The kraut is great paired traditionally with sausages and on sandwiches, but it also is a fun addition to soups and casseroles.

MAKES 6–7 PINTS

Get your boiling-water-bath canning equipment ready and have your jars sterilized and ready.

3 large heads cabbage
1 cup kosher salt

1. Clean the cabbages. Pull off the outer leaves and cut out the core. Discard them. Cut the head into quarters and use a sharp knife or mandoline to slice the cabbage into thin shreds.

2. Using a large stone crock or food-grade plastic container big enough for all of your cabbage, layer a couple of inches of cabbage on the bottom and sprinkle with a little of the salt. Repeat this process, pressing down firmly with your hands every time you add cabbage, until all your cabbage and salt are in the container. Press down really hard one last time to encourage the juices to start releasing.

3. If you are using a crock, place a clean stone weight on top and attach the lid according to the manufacturer's directions. If you are using another container, find a clean plate that will fit inside your container; when the container is almost full, invert the plate on top of the cabbage and press it down. Cover the whole container with a clean, dry cloth.

4. Store the crock or container in a cool (70° to 75°F), dark place for the fermentation stage. Do not refrigerate it. For the first 24 hours, check the container every 4 to 8 hours and, with clean hands, press down on the weight or plate to make sure the cabbage is fully submerged in its juices. Take care to keep the container covered to prevent anything from getting into the kraut that might contaminate the fermentation process.

5. Depending on how fresh and wet the cabbage is when you start, the kraut will take 3 days to a few weeks to fully ferment. Keep it in a place where you will check it every day. Press the weight down if any cabbage is not covered in fluid, and start tasting after 3 days. When it softens and reaches the tang you like, get ready to can it.

6. Using a slotted spoon, evenly distribute the cabbage from the container into hot, sterilized jars. Pack the cabbage in as tightly as you can, then ladle or pour in brine to cover the cabbage completely, leaving $1/2$" of headspace. Gently tap the jars to remove air bubbles.

7. Wipe the rim of each jar carefully with a clean towel to ensure a good seal, and carefully place the lids and rims on.

8. Follow your boiling-water-bath canning process and process for 20 minutes, adjusting for altitude based on the chart on page 24.

kimchi

Now we're fermenting Korean-style. Kimchi is basically another form of kraut—it just has fun, flavorful additions. Remember to keep everything clean and dirt-free so nothing interferes with good clean fermenting. Add the kimchi to your favorite soups and stir-fries, or eat it straight from the jar as a snack.

MAKES 6–7 PINTS

Get your boiling-water-bath canning equipment ready and have your jars sterilized and ready.

3 large heads napa cabbage

1/3 cup kosher salt

1 gallon water

1 bunch scallions, roughly
   chopped

2 large carrots, sliced into
   paper-thin disks

2 small pickling cucumbers,
   peeled and thinly sliced

10 cloves garlic, finely chopped

1/4 cup grated fresh ginger

1/3 cup fish sauce

2 teaspoons red-pepper flakes

1 tablespoon sorghum or
   molasses

1. Clean the cabbages. Pull off the outer leaves and cut out the core. Discard them. Cut the head into quarters and use a sharp knife or mandoline to slice the cabbage into thin shreds.

2. In a large glass or stainless steel bowl, dissolve the salt in the water. Place the cabbage, scallions, carrots, and cucumbers in the water and weigh them down with a large glass bowl to keep them completely submerged. Soak for 2 hours.

3. Drain away the water, then add the garlic, ginger, fish sauce, pepper flakes, and sorghum or molasses. Work everything together really well with your hands to incorporate the flavors and help break down the cabbage.

4. Transfer the mixture to hot, sterilized jars and screw the lids on tight. Store the jars at room temperature (70° to 75°F) for 3 to 4 days.

5. Depending on how fresh and wet the cabbage is when you start, the kimchi will take 3 days to a week to fully ferment. Keep it in a place where you will see it, and check it every day. Use a clean spoon to press down on any vegetables not covered in fluid, and start tasting after 3 days. When it softens and reaches the tang you like, get ready to can it.

6. Empty the contents of the jars into a clean large glass or stainless steel bowl. Use a slotted spoon to stir the kimchi and evenly distribute it to clean, hot, sterilized jars. Pack the vegetables in as tightly as you can, then ladle or pour liquid from the bowl into the jars so that everything is completely submerged. Leave 1/2" of headspace. Gently tap the jars to remove air bubbles.

7. Wipe the rim of each jar carefully with a clean towel to ensure a good seal, and carefully place the lids and rims on.

8. Follow your boiling-water-bath canning process and process for 20 minutes, adjusting for altitude based on the chart on page 24.

asian pickled carrots

These pickles are the shoestring carrots that pop up everywhere at Vietnamese restaurants. They add a great vinegary punch to so many dishes. You can use them as a garnish, on sandwiches, in salads, in soups, and in stir-fries.

MAKES 6–7 PINTS

Get your boiling-water-bath canning equipment ready and have your jars sterilized and ready.

4 pounds carrots

4 cups rice wine vinegar

3 cups water

$1\frac{1}{2}$ cups sugar

6 whole star anise pods

1 tablespoon red-pepper flakes

6 tablespoons finely chopped fresh ginger

3 cloves garlic, finely minced

2 teaspoons kosher salt

1. Using a mandoline or sharp knife, carefully cut the carrots into thin matchstick strips.

2. In a large stainless steel pot over high heat, bring the vinegar, water, sugar, star anise, pepper flakes, ginger, garlic, and salt to a boil, stirring occasionally to dissolve the sugar.

3. Add the carrot sticks to the boiling brine. Bring the liquid back to a boil, cook for 2 minutes, then remove from the heat. Using tongs or a slotted spoon, immediately and carefully divide the carrots among hot, sterilized jars. Pack them as tightly as you can and be sure to get a star anise pod in each jar.

4. Carefully ladle or pour the hot brine to cover the carrots in the jars completely, leaving $\frac{1}{2}$" of headspace. Gently tap the jars to remove air bubbles.

5. Wipe the rim of each jar carefully with a clean towel to ensure a good seal, and carefully place the lids and rims on.

6. Follow your boiling-water-bath canning process and process for 20 minutes, adjusting for altitude based on the chart on page 24.

pickled cherry tomatoes

You can't turn all tomatoes into sauce! This is a fun way to preserve those sweet cherry tomatoes. I always use a mix of colors so the jars look pretty on the shelf, and that also makes things more fun when you are plating them later. This same recipe can be used for full-size ripe and green tomatoes. Just cut them into 1" chunks and directly substitute.

MAKES 4 PINTS

Get your boiling-water-bath canning equipment ready and have your jars sterilized and ready.

4 pints cherry tomatoes
4 cups apple cider vinegar
1 cup water
4 tablespoons sugar
4 tablespoons kosher salt
4 cloves garlic, crushed
2 teaspoons whole peppercorns
8 small sprigs fresh oregano

1. Poke a small hole all the way through each cherry tomato or slice bigger ones in half.

2. In a large stainless steel pot over high heat, bring the vinegar, water, sugar, and salt to a boil, stirring occasionally to dissolve the sugar.

3. Evenly distribute the tomatoes, garlic, peppercorns, and oregano among hot, sterilized jars. Pack the tomatoes in closely but don't squish them.

4. Carefully ladle or pour the hot brine to cover the tomatoes in the jars completely, leaving $1/2$" of headspace. Gently tap the jars to remove air bubbles.

5. Wipe the rim of each jar carefully with a clean towel to ensure a good seal, and carefully place the lids and rims on.

6. Follow your boiling-water-bath canning process and process for 15 minutes, adjusting for altitude based on the chart on page 24.

pickled peppers

I grew up with pickled peppers on the counter as a condiment the same way most people use salt and pepper. It was always right beside the shakers. We used the vinegar from them to season finished servings of greens, peas, beans, soups or to add zest to most any dish while we were cooking. It's a habit I continue today. The recipe below features hot peppers—I like a mix of varieties—but it will work with sweet bell peppers as well. Eat the peppers as a snack or use as a recipe ingredient and keep the vinegar for seasoning other dishes.

MAKES 4 PINTS

Get your boiling-water-bath canning equipment ready and have your jars sterilized and ready.

6 pints small chile peppers, such as serrano or jalapeño, wear plastic gloves when handling

4 cups white vinegar

1 cup water

4 tablespoons sugar

4 tablespoons kosher salt

4 cloves garlic, crushed

4 bay leaves

1. Wearing plastic gloves, core the peppers and remove and discard the seeds. Cut the pepper flesh into 1" strips.

2. In a large stainless steel pot over high heat, bring the vinegar, water, sugar, and salt to a boil, stirring occasionally to dissolve the sugar.

3. Evenly distribute the pepper slices, garlic, and bay leaves among hot, sterilized jars. Pack the peppers in tightly.

4. Carefully ladle or pour the hot brine to cover the peppers in the jars completely, leaving ½" of headspace. Gently tap the jars to remove air bubbles.

5. Wipe the rim of each jar carefully with a clean towel to ensure a good seal, and carefully place the lids and rims on.

6. Follow your boiling-water-bath canning process and process for 10 minutes, adjusting for altitude based on the chart on page 24.

Note: *Be careful working with chile peppers! Wear gloves, and be very careful not to touch your eyes or face without thoroughly washing your hands.*

pickled onions

Cipollini, or pearl, onions are the tiny onions you often see in martini glasses. They are obviously wonderful in a good dirty martini but are also great with sandwiches, in salads, or as an addition to a cheese or meat plate.

MAKES 6–7 HALF-PINTS

Get your boiling-water-bath canning equipment ready and have your jars sterilized and ready.

5½ cups apple cider vinegar

1 cup water

2 cups sugar

4 teaspoons kosher salt

3 pounds peeled whole cipollini or pearl onions

4 teaspoons mustard seeds

2 teaspoons red-pepper flakes

6–7 small sprigs fresh rosemary

1. In a large stainless steel pot over high heat, bring the vinegar, water, sugar, and salt to a boil, stirring occasionally to dissolve the sugar.

2. Evenly distribute the onions, mustard seeds, pepper flakes, and rosemary among hot, sterilized jars. Pack the onions in as tightly as you can.

3. Carefully ladle or pour the hot brine to cover the onions in the jars completely, leaving 1" of headspace. Gently tap the jars to remove air bubbles.

4. Wipe the rim of each jar carefully with a clean towel to ensure a good seal, and carefully place the lids and rims on.

5. Follow your boiling-water-bath canning process and process for 10 minutes, adjusting for altitude based on the chart on page 24.

pickled okra

This is the most Southern pickle of them all. It's also the best way to learn to love okra if you are squeamish due to the rumors that it can be slimy. These pickles are anything but. They are a crunchy delight!

MAKES 4 PINTS

Get your boiling-water-bath canning equipment ready and have your jars sterilized and ready.

1½ pounds fresh okra (3–4 inches long)

4 cups apple cider vinegar

1 cup water

4 tablespoons kosher salt

4 cloves garlic, crushed

4 teaspoons mustard seeds

2 teaspoons dill fronds

2 teaspoons red-pepper flakes

1. Wash the okra and leave it whole. Cut off ¼" of the stem ends, and use the tip of a knife to poke a tiny hole in each pod.
2. In a large stainless steel pot, bring the vinegar, water, and salt to a boil, stirring occasionally.
3. Evenly distribute the okra, garlic, mustard seeds, dill, and pepper flakes among hot, sterilized jars. Pack the okra in tightly.
4. Carefully ladle or pour the hot brine to cover the okra in the jars completely, leaving ½" of headspace. Gently tap the jars to remove air bubbles.

5. Wipe the rim of each jar carefully with a clean towel to ensure a good seal, and carefully place the lids and rims on.
6. Follow your boiling-water-bath canning process and process for 10 minutes, adjusting for altitude based on the chart on page 24.

pickled beets and onions

These are some of the prettiest pickles you will ever make! The beets turn everything a vibrant hot pink. Take the onions out and use them separately for a fun color pop in salads and stir-fries, and eat the beets straight from the jar.

MAKES 8–9 PINTS

Get your boiling-water-bath canning equipment ready and have your jars sterilized and ready.

8 pounds small red beets

6 sweet onions, peeled and thinly sliced

4 cups apple cider vinegar

2 cups water

1 cup sugar

1 tablespoon whole cloves (see Note)

2 teaspoons kosher salt

1. Trim the tops and roots off the beets and scrub well until clean. Slice into $\frac{1}{4}$" disks and place them in a large stainless steel pot. Cover them with water and bring to a boil over medium-high heat. Cook for 10 to 15 minutes, or until the beets just start to get tender. Remove from the heat and drain and discard the water. Add the onions to the pot.

2. In a smaller pot over high heat, bring the vinegar, water, sugar, cloves, and salt to a boil. Once it boils, pour it into the pot with the beets and onions. Place the beets pot back on the stove, bring to a boil, then reduce the heat to medium and simmer for 5 minutes. Remove and discard the cloves. Remove the pot from the heat.

3. Carefully use a slotted spoon or tongs to evenly distribute the beet and onion slices into hot, sterilized jars. Then carefully ladle or pour the hot vinegar solution to cover the beets and onions in each jar completely, leaving $\frac{1}{2}$" of headspace. Gently tap the jars to remove air bubbles.

4. Wipe the rim of each jar carefully with a clean towel to ensure a good seal, and carefully place the lids and rims on.

5. Follow your boiling-water-bath canning process and process for 30 minutes, adjusting for altitude based on the chart on page 24.

Note: *If you wish, place the cloves in an herb bag to make it easier to remove them later.*

sautéed greens with pepper vinegar

I'm pretty sure this dish, or a very similar version, was served at my grandmother's house at least 4 days a week. It's a staple of Southern cooking. Once you taste the salty soulful goodness, you will understand.

MAKES 4–6 SERVINGS

½ pound bacon, cut into
    ½" pieces
2 large cloves garlic, minced
2 pints canned greens
    (page 46), strained
1 tablespoon pepper vinegar
    from Pickled Peppers
    (page 104)
Kosher salt and ground black
    pepper

1. In a large cast-iron skillet over medium heat, cook the bacon until it's almost brown. Transfer the bacon pieces to a plate lined with paper towels to drain.

2. Return the skillet to medium-high heat and cook the garlic in the bacon fat for 1 minute. Carefully add the strained greens: Excess liquid in them may cause the bacon fat to pop. Toss the greens well in the bacon fat and cook for 2 minutes. Add the bacon pieces back in and cook for 2 minutes. You don't have to cook for long—the greens are already cooked, you're just reheating.

3. When the greens are the consistency you want, remove the dish from the heat, drizzle with the vinegar, season with salt and pepper, and serve immediately.

panzanella salad with pickled cherry tomatoes

This lovely salad is hearty enough to be a meal on its own and uses several items from your canning pantry.

MAKES 6–8 SERVINGS

3 tablespoons olive oil, plus
    more as needed

1 small baguette or boule, cut
    into 1" cubes (6 cups total)

1 teaspoon kosher salt

1 pint Pickled Cherry Tomatoes,
    drained (page 103)

1 medium cucumber, peeled and
    sliced into ½"-thick disks

1 red bell pepper, cored, seeded,
    and cut into thin strips

1 small red onion, finely
    chopped

½ cup fresh basil, roughly
    chopped

2 cups arugula, roughly chopped

3 stalks Pickled Okra (page 107),
    sliced into ½"-thick disks

Kosher salt and ground black
    pepper

½ cup Roasted Tomato
    Vinaigrette (page 156)

1. In a large skillet over medium heat, warm the oil. Add the bread and salt and cook, stirring frequently, for 10 minutes, or until the bread is nicely browned. If the pan gets too dry, drizzle in a little more oil.

2. Transfer the browned bread pieces to a large salad bowl. Add the cherry tomatoes, cucumber, bell pepper, onion, basil, arugula, and okra. Season the mixture liberally with salt and black pepper, and drizzle with the vinaigrette. Toss well.

3. Let the salad rest for 15 to 30 minutes before serving.

asian vegetable soup

This is a great soup to make when there's nothing fresh in the house. The recipe calls for fresh Thai basil, but it's delicious without it as well—meaning you can cook this dish completely from the pantry. You can also tweak the recipe as you like. Make it hotter by adding chile peppers or hot sauce, or add meat or mushrooms for a more hearty dish.

MAKES 6–8 SERVINGS

2 quarts Vegetable Broth
   (page 177)
1 pint kimchi (page 100)
1 pint Asian Pickled Carrots
   (page 101), strained
1 half-pint Ginger–Scallion
   Sauce (page 162)
¼ cup Thai basil, roughly
   chopped
Kosher salt and ground black
   pepper
Hot sauce, to serve

1. In a large pot over medium-high heat, cook the broth until it just starts to boil. Stir in the kimchi, carrots, and sauce and cook for 5 minutes.

2. Remove from the heat and stir in the basil. Season to taste with salt and pepper, and serve immediately with hot sauce on the side.

pickles

CHAPTER 4

relish, chutney, and salsa

This collection of recipes makes a fantastic addition to any well-stocked pantry. They are all similar products from different cultures around the world, and we use them in similar ways. My Southern relish isn't all that different from an Indian chutney or a Latin American salsa. All are used to spice up and add special flavors to basic dishes.

Having a steady stash of these recipes in your pantry will make hectic weeknight meals so much easier. You can take a bowl of rice and add any of these recipes, and you will have a comforting and satisfying meal.

Feel free to play with the heat (chile pepper) levels in these recipes. They can always be spiced up by adding an extra chopped hot pepper during the cooking phase.

basic salsa

I make this recipe over and over again every summer. We eat at least a jar a week for snacking, but I also use it as a base for so many dishes—beans and rice, black bean soup, Mexican rice, egg dishes, tacos, fajitas . . . the list goes on and on. Do yourself a favor: Make several batches. Roma tomatoes or a hearty heirloom tomato like a beefsteak make the best salsa.

MAKES 6 PINTS

Get your boiling-water-bath canning equipment ready and have your jars sterilized and ready.

9 pounds tomatoes, cored and peeled

4 large red bell peppers, seeded and chopped

6 red onions, roughly chopped

6 chile peppers (Hungarian wax, serrano, or jalapeño), seeded and chopped, wear plastic gloves when handling

1¼ cups apple cider vinegar

4 cloves garlic, finely chopped

2 tablespoons fresh cilantro, finely chopped

2 tablespoons kosher salt

1 teaspoon red-pepper flakes

1. Peel the tomatoes or process them in a high-powered blender or food processor to break down the skins and seeds. If you are peeling, follow the steps in the recipe on page 40.

2. In a large stainless steel pot, bring the tomatoes, bell peppers, onions, chile peppers, vinegar, garlic, cilantro, salt, and pepper flakes to a boil. Reduce the heat so the ingredients maintain a medium boil and cook for about 60 minutes, depending on how juicy the tomatoes are, or until the volume is reduced to half the original amount.

3. When the salsa has cooked down as much as you want, carefully ladle or pour the salsa into hot, sterilized jars, leaving ½" of headspace. Gently tap the jars to remove air bubbles.

4. Wipe the rim of each jar carefully with a clean towel to ensure a good seal, and carefully place the lids and rims on.

5. Follow your boiling-water-bath canning process and process for 15 minutes, adjusting for altitude based on the chart on page 24.

relish, chutney, and salsa

corn and black bean salsa

This recipe is a variation on basic salsa. The corn and black beans add hearty elements and make for a more substantial dipping salsa. I usually use fresh-off-the-cob or frozen corn, but canned corn will work in a pinch. It will just be softer in the finished product.

MAKES 7 PINTS

Get your boiling-water-bath canning equipment ready and have your jars sterilized and ready.

8 pounds tomatoes, cored and peeled

3 large red bell peppers, seeded and chopped

4 red onions, roughly chopped

4 chile peppers (Hungarian wax, serrano, or jalapeño), seeded and chopped, wear plastic gloves when handling

3 cups corn kernels

3 cups canned black beans, drained and rinsed

1 1/4 cups apple cider vinegar

4 cloves garlic, finely chopped

2 tablespoons fresh cilantro, finely chopped

2 tablespoons kosher salt

1 teaspoon red-pepper flakes

1. Peel the tomatoes or process them in a high-powered blender or food processor to break down the skins and seeds. If you are peeling, follow the steps in the recipe on page 40.

2. In a large stainless steel pot over medium-high heat, bring the tomatoes, bell peppers, onions, chile peppers, corn, beans, vinegar, garlic, cilantro, salt, and pepper flakes to a boil. Reduce the heat so the ingredients maintain a medium boil and cook for about 60 minutes, depending on how juicy the tomatoes are, or until the volume is reduced to half the original amount.

3. When the salsa has cooked down as much as you want, carefully ladle the salsa into hot, sterilized jars, leaving 1/2" of headspace. Gently tap the jars to remove air bubbles.

4. Wipe the rim of each jar carefully with a clean towel to ensure a good seal, and carefully place the lids and rims on.

5. Follow your boiling-water-bath canning process and process for 15 minutes, adjusting for altitude based on the chart on page 24.

basic pickle relish

This recipe is versatile. You can use most any pickle as the base for the relish. The cucumber pickles on pages 90 and 92 work particularly well. Use the relish for potato and egg salads, deviled eggs, or as topping for sandwiches, burgers, or hot dogs.

MAKES 8 HALF-PINTS

Get your boiling-water-bath canning equipment ready and have your jars sterilized and ready.

4 pints pickles (pages 90, 92)
1 cup water

1. Drain the brine from the pickles into a medium bowl. Set the brine aside.

2. For a chunky relish, use a sharp knife to chop the pickles into $\frac{1}{4}$" pieces. For a smoother relish, put the pickles in a food processor and pulse a few times to break down the pickles.

3. Pack the pickles into hot, sterilized jars, leaving $\frac{1}{4}$" of headspace.

4. In a stainless steel pot over high heat, bring the reserved brine and the water to a boil. Remove from the heat and carefully ladle or pour the hot brine to cover the pickles in the jars completely, leaving $\frac{1}{4}$" of headspace. Gently tap the jars to remove air bubbles.

5. Wipe the rim of each jar carefully with a clean towel to ensure a good seal, and carefully place the lids and rims on.

6. Follow your boiling-water-bath canning process and process for 10 minutes, adjusting for altitude based on the chart on page 24.

relish, chutney, and salsa

chowchow

Chowchow is a Southern staple that is like the love child of sweet pickle relish and sauerkraut. Treat it like sauerkraut and use it as a topping on sausages and hot dogs or as a sweet addition to your bowl of cooked greens. You can make a spicy version by substituting 3 chile peppers for one of your sweet bell peppers.

MAKES 8 HALF-PINTS

Get your boiling-water-bath canning equipment ready and have your jars sterilized and ready.

8 large green tomatoes, cored and roughly chopped

8 bell peppers, cored, seeded, and roughly chopped

3 pounds sweet onions, roughly chopped

2 heads cabbage, cored and roughly chopped

1 cup kosher salt

4$\frac{1}{2}$ cups white vinegar

3 cups firmly packed light brown sugar

3 tablespoons pickling spice

1. In a large stainless steel pot, combine the tomatoes, peppers, onions, and cabbage. Cover with the salt. Mix to evenly distribute the salt, then cover everything in the pot with warm tap water. Let the mixture sit at room temperature for 3 to 4 hours (or overnight), until the cabbage starts to soften.

2. Using cheesecloth or a blanching bag, drain the vegetables and press out any excess liquid.

3. In another large stainless steel pot over high heat, bring the vinegar, sugar, and pickling spice to a boil, stirring occasionally to prevent the sugar from sticking. Add the drained vegetables and bring everything to a boil again.

4. Carefully ladle or pour the chowchow into hot, sterilized jars, leaving $\frac{1}{2}$" of headspace. Make sure all the vegetables are fully wet and immersed in liquid. Gently tap the jars to remove air bubbles.

5. Wipe the rim of each jar carefully with a clean towel to ensure a good seal, and carefully place the lids and rims on.

6. Follow your boiling-water-bath canning process and process for 10 minutes, adjusting for altitude based on the chart on page 24.

fig chutney

Chutney is a great item to have in any pantry. It's an easy addition to cheese and meat plates, but it also spices up meat dishes in a flash. Put this chutney on top of a pork roast in the slow cooker, serve with seared chicken breasts, or pair with sharp cheddar cheese crostini.

MAKES 8 HALF-PINTS

Get your boiling-water-bath canning equipment ready and have your jars sterilized and ready.

1 cup raisins

1 cup brandy or cognac

2 cups apple cider vinegar

2 cups firmly packed light brown sugar

8 cups fresh figs, stems removed and quartered

2 large pears, peeled, cored, and diced

2 sweet onions, finely chopped

1$\frac{1}{2}$ teaspoons kosher salt

2 teaspoons grated fresh ginger

1 teaspoon ground cloves

1 teaspoon ground nutmeg

1. In a small bowl, soak the raisins in the brandy or cognac for 20 minutes.

2. In a stainless steel pot over high heat, bring the vinegar and sugar to a boil, stirring occasionally to prevent the sugar from sticking. Add the figs, pears, onions, raisins, salt, cloves, and nutmeg and bring to a boil. Reduce the heat to low and simmer, stirring frequently to prevent sticking, for 1 hour, or until the mixture has thickened to a jamlike consistency.

3. Carefully ladle or pour the chutney into hot, sterilized jars, leaving $\frac{1}{2}$" of headspace. Gently tap the jars to remove air bubbles.

4. Wipe the rim of each jar carefully with a clean towel to ensure a good seal, and carefully place the lids and rims on.

5. Follow your boiling-water-bath canning process and process for 10 minutes, adjusting for altitude based on the chart on page 24.

relish, chutney, and salsa

mango chutney

Mango chutney is sweet and tart. It's a wonderful condiment for a bowl of rice or as a marinade for steaks or pork chops.

MAKES 8 HALF-PINTS

Get your boiling-water-bath canning equipment ready and have your jars sterilized and ready.

1 cup white raisins

1 cup white wine

2 cups white vinegar

2 cups sugar

8 cups fresh mango (6–7 whole), peeled, pitted, and roughly chopped

2 red onions, finely chopped

4 tablespoons grated fresh ginger

1$\frac{1}{2}$ teaspoons kosher salt

1 teaspoon mustard seeds

2 cloves garlic, minced

$\frac{1}{4}$ teaspoon red-pepper flakes

1. In a small bowl, soak the raisins in the white wine for 20 minutes.

2. In a stainless steel pot over high heat, bring the vinegar and sugar to a boil, stirring occasionally to prevent the sugar from sticking. Add the mango, onions, ginger, salt, mustard seeds, garlic, and pepper flakes and return to a boil. Reduce the heat to low and simmer, stirring frequently to prevent sticking, for about 45 minutes, or until the mixture has thickened to a jamlike consistency.

3. Carefully ladle or pour the chutney into hot, sterilized jars, leaving $\frac{1}{2}$" of headspace. Gently tap the jars to remove air bubbles.

4. Wipe the rim of each jar carefully with a clean towel to ensure a good seal, and carefully place the lids and rims on.

5. Follow your boiling-water-bath canning process and process for 15 minutes, adjusting for altitude based on the chart on page 24.

peach salsa

This salsa is a refreshingly sweeter spin on regular salsa. You can serve with chips as a dip or pair as a cold topping for grilled fish or shrimp. The recipe also works well with mango or pineapple as a substitute for the peaches. You just need 8 cups of diced fruit.

MAKES 5–6 PINTS

Get your boiling-water-bath canning equipment ready and have your jars sterilized and ready.

16 medium fresh peaches, peeled, cored, and diced

1–2 tablespoons fresh lime juice

3 medium tomatoes, peeled, cored, and diced

1 small red bell pepper, peeled, seeded, and diced

1 cup sugar

$^3/_4$ cup white vinegar

$^1/_4$ cup fresh cilantro, finely chopped

$^1/_4$ cup fresh basil, finely chopped

3 cloves garlic, minced

1 tablespoon ground cumin

1 tablespoon kosher salt

$^1/_2$ tablespoon smoked paprika

1. In a large glass or stainless steel bowl, combine the peaches and lime juice. Mix to coat, then let the peaches sit in their juices for 30 to 60 minutes, depending on how ripe the peaches are. Let them soak until they just start to get tender.

2. In a large stainless steel pot over medium-high heat, bring the peaches and their juices, the tomatoes, pepper, sugar, vinegar, cilantro, basil, garlic, cumin, salt, and paprika to a boil, stirring regularly to prevent sticking. Boil for 1 minute, then remove from the heat.

3. Carefully ladle or pour the salsa into hot, sterilized jars, leaving $^1/_2$" of headspace. Gently tap the jars to remove air bubbles.

4. Wipe the rim of each jar carefully with a clean towel to ensure a good seal, and carefully place the lids and rims on.

5. Follow your boiling-water-bath canning process and process for 15 minutes, adjusting for altitude based on the chart on page 24.

pepper relish

Pepper relish is basically chopped pickled peppers. You can make it hotter or sweeter by adding or taking away chile peppers. Pepper relish can be used to add flavor in almost any dish and is a wonderful addition to pimento cheese, chicken salad, or potato salad.

MAKES 6–7 HALF-PINTS

Get your boiling-water-bath canning equipment ready and have your jars sterilized and ready.

7–8 large red, yellow, or orange bell peppers, seeded and finely chopped

1 small chile pepper (jalapeño or serrano), seeded and finely chopped, wear plastic gloves when handling

3 medium yellow onions, finely chopped

1$\frac{1}{2}$ cups white vinegar

1 cup sugar

4 teaspoons kosher salt

2 teaspoons mustard seeds

1. In a stainless steel pot over medium-high heat, bring the bell peppers, chile peppers, onions, vinegar, sugar, salt, and mustard seeds to a boil, stirring occasionally to prevent the sugar from sticking. Reduce the heat to low and simmer, stirring frequently to prevent sticking, for 30 minutes.
2. Carefully ladle or pour the hot relish into hot, sterilized jars, leaving $\frac{1}{2}$" of headspace. Gently tap the jars to remove air bubbles.

3. Wipe the rim of each jar carefully with a clean towel to ensure a good seal, and carefully place the lids and rims on.
4. Follow your boiling-water-bath canning process and process for 10 minutes, adjusting for altitude based on the chart on page 24.

relish, chutney, and salsa

salsa verde

Use this salsa the same way you would use a tomato-based salsa—as a dip, on enchiladas or tacos—but you can also use it to spice up basic scrambled eggs or cook chicken thighs or breasts in it and serve over rice. If you can't find tomatillos, you can substitute green tomatoes by weight.

MAKES 8 HALF-PINTS

Get your boiling-water-bath canning equipment ready and have your jars sterilized and ready.

4 pounds tomatillos, peeled, cored, and finely chopped

2 red onions, finely chopped

1 small chile pepper (jalapeño or serrano), seeded and finely chopped, wear plastic gloves when handling

1 cup white vinegar

8 cloves garlic, minced

4 tablespoons fresh cilantro, finely chopped

1–2 tablespoons fresh lime juice

1 tablespoon ground cumin

1 teaspoon kosher salt

1 teaspoon red-pepper flakes

1. In a stainless steel pot over medium-high heat, bring the tomatillos, onions, chile pepper, vinegar, garlic, cilantro, lime juice, cumin, salt, and pepper flakes to a boil, stirring occasionally to prevent sticking. Reduce the heat to low and simmer, stirring frequently to prevent sticking, for 10 minutes.

2. Carefully ladle or pour the salsa into hot, sterilized jars, leaving $1/2$" of headspace. Gently tap the jars to remove air bubbles.

3. Wipe the rim of each jar carefully with a clean towel to ensure a good seal, and carefully place the lids and rims on.

4. Follow your boiling-water-bath canning process and process for 15 minutes, adjusting for altitude based on the chart on page 24.

relish, chutney, and salsa

black bean soup

This soup is a great base for varied meals. If you're hankering for something simple, just have soup. Or you can spice it up with rice and tortillas and add garnishes like sour cream, cheese, chopped chile peppers, and cilantro.

MAKES 4–6 SERVINGS

2 cups dried beans (black, kidney, or pinto)
1 tablespoon kosher salt
1 quart Meat Broth or Vegetable Broth (pages 185, 177)
1 pint Salsa (page 119)
1 teaspoon ground cumin
1 teaspoon chili powder
1 teaspoon smoked paprika
Kosher salt and ground black pepper

1. In a large stainless steel pot, combine the beans and salt. Fill the pot with 6 cups of water, or enough water to cover the beans with several inches of water. (That's 3 cups of water for every cup of dried beans.) Bring the beans to a rolling boil and cook for 2 minutes. Remove from the heat and let the beans soak, covered, in the water for 1 hour.

2. Drain and reserve the soaking liquid.

3. In large stainless steel pot, combine the soaked beans, broth, salsa, cumin, chili powder, paprika, and salt and pepper to taste. The beans should be covered by at least an inch of broth. If they are not, add enough of the soaking water to cover them. Bring the pot to a boil, then reduce the heat to medium and simmer for 30 to 45 minutes, or until the beans are tender and the soup has reached your desired consistency.

4. Serve immediately with your favorite garnishes.

seared lamb chops with mango chutney

This recipe will show like a gourmet meal but will take you less than 10 minutes to prepare. If you don't tell, neither will I.

MAKES 2–3 SERVINGS

3 cloves garlic, finely chopped
1 tablespoon olive oil
2 teaspoons kosher salt
1 teaspoon ground black pepper
6 lamb rib or loin chops
1 half-pint Mango Chutney
   (page 126)

1. Place an oven rack 5" from the broiler unit. Preheat the broiler.
2. In a small bowl, combine the garlic, oil, salt, and pepper. Rub the mixture evenly over the chops. Arrange the chops in a single layer on a broiler pan.

3. Broil the lamb for 3 minutes. Carefully flip the chops and cook for 3 minutes on the other side. Flip one last time, spoon a dollop of chutney on top of each chop, and return to the oven for 2 minutes, or until a thermometer inserted in the center registers 145°F for medium-rare. Cook an additional minute or two, but no more, for well-done chops. Serve immediately.

relish, chutney, and salsa

deviled eggs

I'm Southern. There's lots of things we might have to apologize for. Our deviled eggs aren't one of them. We love them. I had a version in my last cookbook, I'll have a version in my next one. This version is the first one I learned to make. These are basic deviled eggs. Feel free to get creative. Add bacon, chives, chile peppers, little sardines—you dream it, you can do it.

MAKES 24

12 eggs
¹/₂ cup Duke's mayonnaise
3 tablespoons whole grain
    mustard
¹/₄ cup Basic Pickle Relish
    (page 121)
Kosher salt and ground black
    pepper

1. Place the eggs in a single layer in a medium saucepan. Add enough water to cover them by a couple of inches. Bring to a boil, cover, reduce the heat to low, and cook for 1 minute. Remove the pan from the heat and leave it covered for about 15 minutes. Drain the water, and carefully place the eggs in a bowl of ice water.
2. The easiest way to peel the eggs is under a stream of cool running water. Gently crack the shells and peel in the stream of water. Slice the peeled eggs in half and scoop out the yolks. Place the yolks in a small mixing bowl and set the whites on your serving plate.

3. Add the mayonnaise, mustard, and relish to the bowl with the yolks. Mash the yolks well and whip everything together. Season to taste with salt and pepper.
4. Evenly disperse heaping spoonfuls of the mixture into the egg whites, or use a pastry bag to pipe the mixture into the eggs for a more finished look. You can garnish with a few extra pieces of relish or a scatter of finishing salt. Serve immediately or refrigerate for later.

CHAPTER 5

sauces, butters, and marinades

My wintertime kitchen revolves around recipes in this section. We love slow-roasted dishes and savory flavors. I depend on preserved items from summer to keep those dishes varied and delicious. The tomato sauce alone in this section can be used 100 different ways. Go ahead and plan on making many of these recipes in bulk. You'll want to have a lot on hand.

roasted tomato sauce

This is the most versatile item in my pantry. I make hundreds of pints a year. It's a perfectly simple tomato base for so many other recipes. You can use it straight out of the jar as a dipping sauce, as a base for your favorite pasta and pizza dishes, when braising meats, or as the base for tomato soup. Note: If your tomatoes were heavily watered or recently rained on, you will have a lot of liquid and the finished product may look separated in the jars. The tomato sauce will reincorporate when the jars are shaken or reheated later for consumption.

MAKES 4 PINTS

Get your pressure-canning equipment ready and have your jars sterilized and ready.

$\frac{1}{4}$ cup olive oil

8 pounds very ripe tomatoes, cut into quarters

1 sweet onion, cut into quarters

2 teaspoons kosher salt

1 teaspoon ground black pepper

1. Preheat the oven to 400°F.

2. Pour half of the oil onto a large baking sheet and spread it around. Place the tomatoes on the oiled sheet. Break the onion quarters into pieces and sprinkle them, along with the salt and pepper, evenly over the tomatoes and then dress everything with the remaining oil.

3. Roast for about 45 minutes, or until the tomato skins start to wrinkle.

4. Transfer the mixture to a high-powered blender or heavy-duty food processor and puree until smooth.

5. Carefully ladle or pour the sauce into hot, sterilized jars, leaving $\frac{1}{4}$" of headspace. Gently tap the jars to remove air bubbles.

6. Wipe the rim of each jar carefully with a clean towel to ensure a good seal, and carefully place the lids and rims on.

7. Follow your pressure-canning process and process 10 pounds of pressure for 20 minutes, adjusting for altitude based on the chart on page 24.

sauces, butters, and marinades

marinara sauce

This sauce is a traditional marinara recipe. It's more refined than the roasted tomato sauce on the previous page and is suitable in traditional Italian and Greek dishes that call for a tomato sauce.

MAKES 6 TO 8 PINTS

Get your pressure-canning equipment ready and have your jars sterilized and ready.

20 pounds whole tomatoes

2 tablespoons olive oil

2 medium sweet onions, finely chopped

2 large red bell peppers, cored, seeded, and finely chopped

6 cloves garlic, minced

1/2 cup red wine

1/4 cup firmly packed light brown sugar

1 cup fresh basil, roughly chopped

1/4 cup fresh oregano, roughly chopped

4 teaspoons salt

2 teaspoons ground black pepper

1. Fill a large bowl with ice water and set it to the side. Bring a large pot of water to a boil. Working in batches, drop tomatoes into the boiling water a few at a time and blanch for 30 to 60 seconds, or until you see the skin start to wrinkle and split. Using a slotted spoon, immediately and carefully move them to the ice water. Let them cool in the water for 1 minute before peeling them with your fingers. Repeat until all the tomatoes are peeled.

2. Cut the peeled tomatoes into quarters and place them in a large stainless steel pot. Bring the tomatoes to a boil, reduce the heat to medium, and simmer, stirring regularly to prevent sticking, for 20 minutes. Use a potato masher or ricer to crush the tomatoes.

3. Meanwhile, in a large skillet over medium-high heat, warm the oil. Add the onions, bell peppers, and garlic and cook for 5 to 7 minutes, or until the onions are translucent. Stir the onion mixture into the tomatoes, then add the wine, sugar, basil, oregano, salt, and black pepper. Increase the heat and bring to a boil, stirring often. Reduce the heat to medium-low and simmer uncovered, again stirring often, for 10 to 20 minutes, or until the sauce is as thick as you want it.

4. Carefully ladle or pour the sauce into hot, sterilized jars, leaving 1/4" of headspace. Gently tap the jars to remove air bubbles.

5. Wipe the rim of each jar carefully with a clean towel to ensure a good seal, and carefully place the lids and rims on.

6. Follow your pressure-canning process and process at 10 pounds of pressure for 20 minutes, adjusting for altitude based on the chart on page 24.

pear butter

This recipe is wonderful to whip up in large batches. It's pretty simple and makes a great hostess gift at the holidays. It is delicious spread on toast or biscuits and is also a great marinade for slow-cooker pork roast. You can substitute apples directly for pears to make an apple butter or combine the two for a delicious pear-apple butter!

MAKES 6 HALF-PINTS

Get your boiling-water-bath canning equipment ready and have your jars sterilized and ready.

4 pounds fresh pears, peeled, cored, and quartered

2 cups water

4 cups sugar

2 teaspoons ground cinnamon

$\frac{1}{4}$ teaspoon ground cloves

1. In a large stainless steel pot over medium heat, combine the pears and water and simmer, stirring regularly, until the pears soften.

2. Use an immersion blender to puree the fruit in the pot. Alternatively, transfer the mixture to a food processor to puree, then return the puree to the pot. Stir in the sugar, cinnamon, and cloves and cook over medium heat, stirring constantly, until the sugar dissolves. Increase the heat to medium-high and cook at a low boil, stirring frequently, for 20 to 30 minutes, or until the mixture is thick enough to mound on a spoon.

3. Carefully ladle or pour the hot butter into hot, sterilized jars, leaving $\frac{1}{4}$" of headspace. Gently tap the jars to remove air bubbles.

4. Wipe the rim of each jar carefully with a clean towel to ensure a good seal, and carefully place the lids and rims on.

5. Follow your boiling-water-bath canning process and process for 10 minutes, adjusting for altitude based on the chart on page 24.

sauces, butters, and marinades

ginger-pineapple butter

This recipe is a fun tropical spin on traditional fruit butters. The ginger gives it a nice zing. Use it as a marinade as is for chicken skewers on the grill, or thin some using soy sauce or any type of meat or vegetable broth and serve over rice.

MAKES 6–7 HALF-PINTS

Get your boiling-water-bath canning equipment ready and have your jars sterilized and ready.

4 pounds fresh pineapple, peeled and cut into 1" cubes

2 apples, peeled, cored, and quartered

3 tablespoons fresh lemon juice

2 cups water

3 tablespoons grated fresh ginger

4 cups sugar

1. In a large stainless steel pot over medium heat, combine the pineapple, apples, lemon juice, and water and cook at a simmer, stirring regularly, until the fruit softens.

2. Use an immersion blender to puree the fruit in the pot. Alternatively, transfer the mixture to a food processor to puree, then return the puree to the pot. Stir in the ginger and sugar and cook over medium heat, stirring constantly, until the sugar dissolves. Increase the heat to medium-high and cook at a low boil, stirring frequently, for 20 to 30 minutes, or until the mixture is thick enough to mound on a spoon.

3. Carefully ladle or pour the hot butter into hot, sterilized jars, leaving $1/4$" of headspace. Gently tap the jars to remove air bubbles.

4. Wipe the rim of each jar carefully with a clean towel to ensure a good seal, and carefully place the lids and rims on.

5. Follow your boiling-water-bath canning process and process for 10 minutes, adjusting for altitude based on the chart on page 24.

applesauce

I make HUGE batches of applesauce every year. It's a great snack straight out of the jar for all ages. A jar of applesauce has saved the day at many group gatherings—even the pickiest eater will eat a bowl of homemade applesauce and go away happy.

MAKES 6 PINTS

Get your boiling-water-bath canning equipment ready and have your jars sterilized and ready.

8 pounds heirloom apples, peeled, cored, and cut into quarters

3 tablespoons fresh lemon juice

2 cups water

6 tablespoons firmly packed dark brown sugar

1 teaspoon ground cinnamon

1. In a large stainless steel pot over medium-high heat, combine the apples, lemon juice, and water and bring to a boil. Reduce the heat to medium-low, add the sugar and cinnamon, and simmer for 25 to 30 minutes, or until the apples have completely softened. Stir often to prevent sticking. Cooking time will depend on how moist the apples are, so watch your pot and adjust as you go.

2. When the apples are as soft as you want, remove the pot from the heat and mash the apples with a potato masher or ricer until the sauce is the desired consistency. You can also use an immersion blender for a super-smooth sauce.

3. Carefully ladle or pour the hot sauce into hot, sterilized jars, leaving $\frac{1}{4}$" of headspace. Gently tap the jars to remove air bubbles.

4. Wipe the rim of each jar carefully with a clean towel to ensure a good seal, and carefully place the lids and rims on.

5. Follow your boiling-water-bath canning process and process for 10 minutes, adjusting for altitude based on the chart on page 24.

sauces, butters, and marinades

soy vinegar dipping sauce

This sauce is the best for dipping Asian–style dumplings, but it's a wonderful marinade for chicken, pork, and beef, too. You can also drizzle it on plain rice or noodles to spice them up a bit.

MAKES 4 HALF-PINTS

Get your boiling-water-bath canning equipment ready and have your jars sterilized and ready.

2 cups soy sauce

2 cups rice vinegar

4 teaspoons toasted sesame oil

3 tablespoons Asian hot sauce (like Sriracha)

1 tablespoon grated fresh ginger

1. In a large stainless steel pot, bring the soy sauce, vinegar, oil, hot sauce, and ginger to a boil.

2. Carefully ladle or pour the hot sauce into hot, sterilized jars, leaving $1/4$" of headspace. Gently tap the jars to remove air bubbles.

3. Wipe the rim of each jar carefully with a clean towel to ensure a good seal, and carefully place the lids and rims on.

4. Follow your boiling–water-bath canning process and process for 10 minutes, adjusting for altitude based on the chart on page 24.

soy-ginger "teriyaki" marinade

This "teriyaki" sauce was born of necessity when one of our sons started dating a young woman with celiac disease, and she couldn't consume anything with gluten. We love teriyaki as a marinade on most anything, so I needed something that was safe for her. This is safe—and so much more delicious than any store-bought option I've tried.

MAKES 5 HALF-PINTS

Get your boiling-water-bath canning equipment ready and have your jars sterilized and ready.

2 cups tamari (gluten-free soy sauce)

2 cups firmly packed light brown sugar

1 cup rice vinegar

4 tablespoons grated fresh ginger

2 tablespoons apple juice

2 tablespoons fresh lime juice

1. In a large stainless steel pot over medium heat, bring the tamari, sugar, vinegar, ginger, apple juice, and lime juice to a boil. Reduce the heat to low and simmer, stirring often to keep the sugar from sticking, for 15 minutes.

2. Carefully ladle or pour the hot sauce into hot, sterilized jars, leaving $1/4$" of headspace. Gently tap the jars to remove air bubbles.

3. Wipe the rim of each jar carefully with a clean towel to ensure a good seal, and carefully place the lids and rims on.

4. Follow your boiling-water-bath canning process and process for 15 minutes, adjusting for altitude based on the chart on page 24.

sauces, butters, and marinades

ratatouille

In our house, ratatouille does double duty as a sauce and a side. You can serve it over pasta, polenta, or rice to make a main dish, or just heat it up and serve as a stand-alone side dish with your favorite main course.

MAKES 5–6 PINTS

Get your pressure-canning equipment ready and have your jars sterilized and ready.

5 tablespoons olive oil, divided

1 pound eggplant, cut into 1" chunks

1 pound zucchini, cut into 1" chunks

3 medium sweet onions, roughly chopped

3 large meaty tomatoes (like Oxheart or a beefsteak), cored and roughly chopped

2 large red bell peppers, cored, seeded, and cut into 1" chunks

5 cloves garlic, minced

¼ cup fresh basil leaves, roughly chopped

2 teaspoons fresh thyme leaves

2 teaspoons fresh oregano leaves

Kosher salt and ground black pepper

1. Preheat the oven to 400°F. Coat a large baking sheet with 2 tablespoons of the oil.

2. Spread the eggplant, zucchini, onions, tomatoes, and bell peppers on the prepared baking sheet. Drizzle another 2 tablespoons of oil over the vegetables and stir to coat. Roast for about 45 minutes, or until the tomato skins start to wrinkle.

3. In a large stainless steel pot over medium heat, warm the remaining 1 tablespoon oil. Add the garlic and cook for almost a minute, then add the roasted vegetables, basil, thyme, oregano, and salt and pepper to taste. Cook, stirring often, for 15 minutes, until the vegetables have broken down and everything is incorporated. When the ratatouille reaches the consistency you want, remove the pot from the heat.

4. Carefully ladle or pour the hot ratatouille into hot, sterilized jars, leaving 1" of headspace. Gently tap the jars to remove air bubbles.

5. Wipe the rim of each jar carefully with a clean towel to ensure a good seal, and carefully place the lids and rims on.

6. Follow your pressure-canning process and process at 10 pounds of pressure for 30 minutes, adjusting for altitude based on the chart on page 24.

roasted pepper sauce

This sauce is great for those nights when you need a quick pasta dish but are tired of regular tomato sauce. The peppers have a sweet flavor, and the sauce pairs wonderfully with lamb or chicken.

MAKES 3–4 PINTS

Get your boiling-water-bath canning equipment ready and have your jars sterilized and ready.

7 pounds bell peppers, cored, seeded, and cut into strips

1½ pounds Roma tomatoes, cored and cut into 1" chunks

1 small sweet onion, roughly chopped

2 cloves garlic, roughly chopped

¾ cup red wine vinegar

3 tablespoons fresh basil, finely chopped

1 tablespoon sugar

1 teaspoon kosher salt

1. Preheat the oven to 425°F.

2. Spread the peppers, tomatoes, onion, and garlic in a roasting pan and roast, occasionally stirring things around, for 30 to 40 minutes, or until the peppers and tomatoes start to blister and brown. Transfer the pan to a rack to cool.

3. Once the vegetables have cooled partially, but not completely, transfer them to a metal bowl and puree with an immersion blender. Alternatively, put the vegetables in a high-powered blender or food processor in batches and process thoroughly.

4. In a large pot over medium-high heat, combine the pureed mix with the vinegar, basil, sugar, and salt. Bring to a boil, stirring often to prevent sticking, then reduce the heat to low and simmer for 15 to 20 minutes, or until the sauce has reached the thickness you are looking for. Remove from the heat.

5. Carefully ladle or pour the hot sauce into hot, sterilized jars, leaving ½" of headspace. Gently tap the jars to remove air bubbles.

6. Wipe the rim of each jar carefully with a clean towel to ensure a good seal, and carefully place the lids and rims on.

7. Follow your boiling-water-bath canning process and process for 15 minutes, adjusting for altitude based on the chart on page 24.

sauces, butters, and marinades

caponata

We eat a lot of pasta at our house—farmhands are always hungry after a long day of work. I don't want them eating the same sauce all the time, so I mix it up as much as I can. This sauce is very eggplant forward, so you get a little more pleasant bitterness. While great on pasta, it's also wonderful as a sauce for seared chicken breasts.

MAKES 6 PINTS

Get your pressure-canning equipment ready and have your jars sterilized and ready.

1/2 cup olive oil, divided

4 large eggplants, cut into
   1" chunks

4 medium sweet onions, roughly
   chopped

5 cloves garlic, minced

1 cup finely diced celery

4 cups Roasted Tomato Sauce
   (page 141)

1 cup pitted green olives,
   coarsely chopped

1 cup pitted black olives,
   coarsely chopped

1/2 cup red wine vinegar

4 tablespoons firmly packed
   light brown sugar

1/4 cup fresh parsley leaves,
   roughly chopped

2 teaspoons fresh thyme leaves

2 teaspoons fresh oregano leaves

Kosher salt and ground black
   pepper

1. In a large stainless steel pot over medium heat, warm 1/4 cup of the oil. Add the eggplants and cook for 10 minutes, stirring often. Add the onions, garlic, celery, and the remaining 1/4 cup of oil and cook for about 7 minutes, or until the onions are translucent.

2. Add the tomato sauce, olives, vinegar, sugar, parsley, thyme, and oregano and season to taste with salt and pepper. Reduce the heat to low and simmer, covered, for 50 minutes. Stir occasionally to prevent sticking.

3. Uncover the pan and cook for at least 10 minutes so that the juices evaporate. You want this to be a thick sauce—one that the spoon can almost stand up in. The final cooking time will depend on how much moisture was in the raw vegetables. When you have the consistency you want, remove the pot from the heat.

4. Carefully ladle or pour the hot caponata into hot, sterilized jars, leaving 1" of headspace. Gently tap the jars to remove air bubbles.

5. Wipe the rim of each jar carefully with a clean towel to ensure a good seal, and carefully place the lids and rims on.

6. Follow your pressure-canning process and process at 10 pounds of pressure for 30 minutes, adjusting for altitude based on the chart on page 24.

raspberry vinaigrette

This light vinaigrette is perfect in its traditional role as a salad dressing, but it also serves as a delicious marinade for chicken and pork—think pretty pink pork chops! Or if you are feeling more adventurous, drizzle it on raw oysters for sweet-tangy oyster shooters.

MAKES 5–6 HALF-PINTS

Get your boiling-water-bath canning equipment ready and have your jars sterilized and ready.

2½ pounds fresh raspberries

½ cup water

1 cup sugar

⅔ cup white vinegar

6 tablespoons balsamic vinegar

3 tablespoons whole-grain mustard

½ teaspoon fresh thyme

1. In a wide saucepan over medium-high heat, bring the berries and water to a boil. Reduce the heat to low and simmer, uncovered, for 10 minutes, or until the berries soften. Remove the pan from the heat to cool.

2. Once the mixture has cooled partially, but not completely, transfer it to a metal bowl and puree with an immersion blender. Alternatively, put the mixture in a high-powered blender or food processor and process thoroughly. For a smoother product, push the pureed berries through a fine sieve or food mill.

3. Return the puree to the saucepan and stir in the sugar, white vinegar, balsamic vinegar, mustard, and thyme. Bring to a boil over medium-high heat, stirring often to prevent sticking. Cook for 3 minutes, then remove from the heat.

4. Carefully ladle or pour the hot vinaigrette into hot, sterilized jars, leaving ¼" of headspace. Gently tap the jars to remove air bubbles.

5. Wipe the rim of each jar carefully with a clean towel to ensure a good seal, and carefully place the lids and rims on.

6. Follow your boiling-water-bath canning process and process for 10 minutes, adjusting for altitude based on the chart on page 24.

sauces, butters, and marinades

roasted tomato vinaigrette

I could happily drink this vinaigrette straight from the jar. That may not be the best idea, so use it to dress your salads and pasta dishes or as a dipping sauce for bread.

MAKES 8 HALF-PINTS

Get your boiling-water-bath canning equipment ready and have your jars sterilized and ready.

4 pounds very ripe tomatoes, cored and cut into 1" chunks

1/4 cup olive oil

1 cup white vinegar

1/4 cup balsamic vinegar

2 tablespoons fresh lemon juice

4 cloves garlic, minced

1 tablespoon fresh oregano, finely chopped

1 tablespoon fresh basil, finely chopped

2 teaspoons kosher salt

1. Preheat the oven to 425°F.

2. Spread the tomatoes in a roasting pan, drizzle with the oil, and roast, stirring occasionally, for 40 to 45 minutes, or until the tomatoes start to blister and brown. Transfer the pan to a rack to cool.

3. Once the tomatoes have cooled partially, but not completely, transfer them to a metal bowl and puree with an immersion blender. Alternatively, put the tomatoes in a high-powered blender or food processor and process thoroughly. For a smoother product, push the pureed tomatoes through a fine sieve or food mill and discard the seeds and skins.

4. In a large pot over medium heat, bring the pureed tomatoes, white vinegar, balsamic vinegar, lemon juice, garlic, oregano, basil, and salt to a boil, stirring often to prevent sticking. Cook for 3 minutes, then remove from the heat.

5. Carefully ladle or pour the hot vinaigrette into hot, sterilized jars, leaving 1/4" of headspace. Gently tap the jars to remove air bubbles.

6. Wipe the rim of each jar carefully with a clean towel to ensure a good seal, and carefully place the lids and rims on.

7. Follow your boiling-water-bath canning process and process for 20 minutes, adjusting for altitude based on the chart on page 24.

cranberry sauce

You'll never buy the grocery-store canned version of cranberry sauce ever again after you try this recipe. It's light and doesn't have the cloying sweetness the store-bought versions have. Serve it on your Thanksgiving table as a side or use it year-round as a condiment for sandwiches or an addition to your meat and cheese boards.

MAKES 8 HALF-PINTS

Get your boiling-water-bath canning equipment ready and have your jars sterilized and ready.

4 cups granulated sugar

4 cups water

8 cups fresh cranberries

2 tablespoons finely grated orange peel (from 1 large orange)

1. In a large stainless steel pot over high heat, combine the sugar and water and bring to a boil, stirring regularly to dissolve the sugar. Boil for 5 minutes, then add the cranberries and return to a rolling boil. Reduce the heat to medium-low and boil gently, stirring often, for about 15 minutes, or until all the berries burst and the liquid starts to thicken. Stir in the orange peel and cook for 1 minute. Remove from the heat.

2. Carefully ladle or pour the hot sauce into hot, sterilized jars, leaving $\frac{1}{4}$" of headspace. Gently tap the jars to remove air bubbles.

3. Wipe the rim of each jar carefully with a clean towel to ensure a good seal, and carefully place the lids and rims on.

4. Follow your boiling-water-bath canning process and process for 15 minutes, adjusting for altitude based on the chart on page 24.

sauces, butters, and marinades

barbecue sauce— the red kind

In my world, there are multiple kinds of barbecue sauce. There are the yellow and white versions that we turn our nose up at. And there are the two we eat. One is vinegar based and is reserved for pork. The other is red and tomato based and can be smeared on anything that will stay still long enough to get basted. This is the red one. It loves chicken legs cooked on a hot charcoal grill. And you get to use the Roasted Tomato Sauce from last summer as the base!

MAKES 5–6 PINTS

Get your boiling-water-bath canning equipment ready and have your jars sterilized and ready.

5 pints Roasted Tomato Sauce (page 141)

$1\frac{1}{2}$ cups firmly packed light brown sugar

1 cup apple cider vinegar

$\frac{1}{3}$ cup fresh lemon juice

2 tablespoons kosher salt

2 tablespoons dry mustard

4 cloves garlic, finely chopped

1 tablespoon red-pepper flakes

1 tablespoon celery seeds

1. In a large pot over medium-high heat, bring the tomato sauce, sugar, vinegar, lemon juice, salt, mustard, garlic, pepper flakes, and celery seeds to a boil, stirring often to prevent sticking. Reduce the heat to low and simmer, stirring often, for 10 to 20 minutes, or until the mixture cooks down to the desired texture. Remove from the heat.

2. Carefully ladle or pour the hot sauce into hot, sterilized jars, leaving $\frac{1}{4}$" of headspace. Gently tap the jars to remove air bubbles.

3. Wipe the rim of each jar carefully with a clean towel to ensure a good seal, and carefully place the lids and rims on.

4. Follow your boiling-water-bath canning process and process for 20 minutes, adjusting for altitude based on the chart on page 24.

barbecue sauce— eastern north carolina— style

This is the sauce for pork. And by pork, I mean whole-hog barbecue cooked over real wood coals until we can pull the meat right off the bone. Then we douse it with this tangy sauce, and all is right with the world.

MAKES 5 HALF-PINTS

Get your boiling-water-bath canning equipment ready and have your jars sterilized and ready.

5 cups apple cider vinegar
$1/4$ cup firmly packed light
    brown sugar
4 tablespoons kosher salt
1 tablespoon ground red pepper
1 tablespoon red-pepper flakes

1. In a large pot over medium-high heat, bring the vinegar, sugar, salt, red pepper, and pepper flakes to a boil, stirring often to prevent sticking. Remove from the heat.
2. Carefully ladle or pour the hot sauce into hot, sterilized jars, leaving $1/4$" of headspace. Gently tap the jars to remove air bubbles.

3. Wipe the rim of each jar carefully with a clean towel to ensure a good seal, and carefully place the lids and rims on.
4. Follow your boiling-water-bath canning process and process for 10 minutes, adjusting for altitude based on the chart on page 24.

sauces, butters, and marinades

ginger-scallion sauce

This recipe evolved from one I discovered in a magazine and became obsessed with. It's delicious on so many things, serving as a marinade, a dipping sauce for almost anything, or as a dressing for cooked rice, noodles, or meat. I got tired of the chopping every time to make fresh sauce, so I tweaked things a little to make a recipe that could be canned. If you are using the recipe immediately, you can skip the boiling step.

MAKES 4–5 HALF-PINTS

Get your boiling-water-bath canning equipment ready and have your jars sterilized and ready.

9–10 fresh scallions

$\frac{1}{2}$ cup sunflower oil

$\frac{1}{2}$ cup toasted sesame oil

$\frac{1}{4}$ cup finely grated fresh ginger

$\frac{1}{4}$ cup rice wine vinegar

$\frac{1}{4}$ cup soy sauce

1 teaspoon kosher salt

1. Slice the scallions very thinly—paper-thin, if possible. Use the entire scallion, all the way up. You should have 3 cups. Place them in a heatproof metal bowl.

2. In a small saucepan over medium heat, warm the sunflower oil and sesame oil until they just start to pop or smoke. Immediately pour the oils over the chopped scallions. Set aside for 45 to 60 minutes to marinate and cool.

3. In a medium pot over medium-high heat, bring the ginger, vinegar, soy sauce, and salt to a boil, stirring often to prevent sticking. Stir in the scallion mixture and boil for 1 minute. Remove from the heat.

4. Carefully ladle or pour the hot sauce into hot, sterilized jars, leaving $\frac{1}{4}$" of headspace. Gently tap the jars to remove air bubbles.

5. Wipe the rim of each jar carefully with a clean towel to ensure a good seal, and carefully place the lids and rims on.

6. Follow your boiling-water-bath canning process and process for 15 minutes, adjusting for altitude based on the chart on page 24.

roasted red pepper soup

This soup is reminiscent of tomato soup and is just as comforting. The peppers are a little sweeter than tomatoes, though, so it's nice to serve it with something creamy to balance out the sweetness. I like to use chicken broth, but vegetable broth also works.

MAKES 3–4 SERVINGS

1 large sweet onion, finely
   chopped
2 large cloves garlic
2 tablespoons olive oil
2 tablespoons unsalted butter
2 tablespoons all-purpose flour
3 cups Meat Broth (see Note)
   or Vegetable Broth
   (pages 185, 177)
2 pints Roasted Pepper Sauce
   (page 151)
1 tablespoon dried oregano
1 teaspoon sugar
Kosher salt and ground
   black pepper
Sour cream or ricotta cheese,
   for serving

1. In a food processor, puree the onion and garlic.

2. In a medium stainless steel pot over medium–low heat, warm the oil and butter until the butter melts. Add the onion mixture and cook for 4 minutes, stirring constantly to keep it from sticking. Add the flour and stir vigorously to make a roux. Cook for 1 minute, then add the broth, pepper sauce, oregano, and sugar. Season with salt and black pepper to taste. Bring to a simmer over medium heat, stirring regularly to make sure the flour and pepper pulp are not sticking to the bottom.

Reduce the heat to low and cook for 20 minutes, stirring often, until the mixture cooks down to the consistency of tomato soup.

3. Serve immediately with a healthy dollop of sour cream or ricotta cheese and an extra sprinkle of salt and black pepper.

Note: *For this dish, use Meat Broth that has been prepared with chicken.*

meatballs in marinara sauce

This is a quick use of your already canned marinara sauce and makes for a hearty, warming meal on cold winter nights.

MAKES 3–4 SERVINGS

1 pound ground beef
1 pound ground pork
½ cup grated Parmesan cheese, plus extra for garnish
1 large egg
1 cup dried bread crumbs
6 cloves garlic, minced
1 teaspoon dried oregano
1 teaspoon dried basil
1 teaspoon kosher salt
1 teaspoon ground black pepper
¼ cup olive oil
2 pints Marinara Sauce (page 142)
Cooked pasta or polenta, for serving

1. In a large bowl, combine the beef, pork, Parmesan, egg, bread crumbs, garlic, oregano, basil, salt, and pepper, using your hands to make sure all the ingredients are evenly distributed. Roll into balls a little smaller than a golf ball.

2. In a large skillet over medium heat, warm the oil. Cook the meatballs in batches for about 2 minutes per side, or until they are browned and crisp on the outside. Set the meatballs on paper towels to drain. Repeat until all of the meatballs are cooked.

3. Pour the marinara sauce into the same skillet and stir to mix with the meatball drippings. Return the meatballs to the pan and stir to coat with sauce. Reduce the heat to low, cover, and simmer for 10 minutes.

4. Serve immediately with cooked pasta or polenta and an extra sprinkle of Parmesan.

barbecued pork chops

I'm getting a little wild with this recipe, using red barbecue sauce on pork, but I promise: It is delicious. This sauce makes everything taste good—even grilled vegetables!

MAKES 4 SERVINGS

3 cloves garlic, finely chopped

2 tablespoons olive oil

2 tablespoons kosher salt

1 tablespoon ground black pepper

4 pork chops, 1" thick

1 pint Barbecue Sauce—The Red Kind (page 158)

1. In a small bowl, combine the garlic, oil, salt, and pepper. Rub the mixture evenly over the chops. Set the chops aside to rest while you prepare the grill.

2. Coat a grill rack with cooking spray. For a charcoal grill, prepare one dense layer of hot coals. For a gas grill, preheat until the grates are good and hot.

3. Grill the chops for 5 minutes on each side, then brush each side liberally with the barbecue sauce and cook for 2 minutes on each side, or until a thermometer inserted in the center of a chop registers 160°F and the juices run clear. You'll have a nice crusty sear on the outside and a moist, pink center.

4. Let chops rest for a few minutes before serving and accompany with additional barbecue sauce for dipping.

sauces, butters, and marinades

CHAPTER 6

juices
and
soups

Making your own fruit juice at home is a revelation! Store-bought juices can't hold a candle to juice you make yourself. Even after the juice is canned, it retains so much of the fresh fruit flavor that is lost in mass-production juices. You, and your kids, will love having these on hand, ready to drink.

The soups in this section are also great to have on hand. They make meals so much easier. Simply open a jar, quickly reheat, and you have a meal on the table.

Note: When you are making the juices in this section, you need to heat them to the point that they are pasteurized, so keep a thermometer handy. You must be certain that you get temperatures just over 190°F so that any bacteria are killed.

grape juice

Who doesn't love grape juice? This is a wonderful way to preserve grapes if you are lucky enough to have access to lots of fresh grapes. So plant some grapevines, or find a friend with some, and get picking!

MAKES 5–6 QUARTS

Get your boiling-water-bath canning equipment ready and have your jars sterilized and ready.

20 pounds Concord grapes, washed and stemmed
1 cup sugar

1. Bring 4 quarts of water to a boil.

2. Place the grapes in a large stainless steel pot. Add just enough boiling water to cover the grapes. Bring the grapes to a simmer over medium heat and cook for 10 minutes, or until the skins soften.

3. Strain the grapes and their juice through a fine sieve, damp cheesecloth, or a food mill set over a large stainless steel pot or a glass, ceramic, or stainless steel bowl. Discard the solids. Store the juice in the refrigerator for 24 hours.

4. As the juice cools, sediment will settle on the bottom. After 24 hours, carefully pour the clear part of the juice into a large stainless steel pot. Discard the sediment. Add the sugar to the pot and bring to a boil over medium-high heat, stirring regularly to dissolve the sugar. Make sure the temperature gets just over 190°F. Remove from the heat.

5. Carefully ladle or pour the hot juice into hot, sterilized jars, leaving ¼" of headspace. Gently tap the jars to remove air bubbles.

6. Wipe the rim of each jar carefully with a clean towel to ensure a good seal, and carefully place the lids and rims on.

7. Follow your boiling-water-bath canning process and process for 5 minutes, adjusting for altitude based on the chart on page 24.

tomato juice

I had a great-uncle who made tomato juice compulsively, all summer, every summer. It was even the theme of his funeral. Every single person there had been the recipient of a jar of that juice at one point or another. We all knew it meant he loved us. So here's some love in a jar. It's good for you if you drink it straight, and it's a great base for soups and cocktails.

MAKES 8 PINTS

Get your boiling-water-bath canning equipment ready and have your jars sterilized and ready.

15 pounds tomatoes
1/2 cup fresh lemon juice
1 tablespoon kosher salt

1. Core the tomatoes and cut them into quarters, collecting the juices as you work. Place the tomatoes and their juices in a large stainless steel pot and bring to a boil over medium-high heat. Stir often and chop at the tomatoes while you are stirring to help break them down. Reduce the heat to medium-low and simmer, stirring and chopping frequently, for 15 minutes, or until the tomatoes are completely broken down.

2. Strain the tomatoes through a sieve or food mill set over a large pot or bowl. Discard the seeds and skins (or save for dehydrating into tomato powder later) and capture the juice. Return the strained juice to the pot and add the lemon juice.

Increase the heat to medium and bring to a strong rolling boil. Make sure the temperature gets just over 190°F. Remove from the heat and stir in the salt.

3. Carefully ladle or pour the hot juice into hot, sterilized jars, leaving 1/2" of headspace. Gently tap the jars to remove air bubbles.

4. Wipe the rim of each jar carefully with a clean towel to ensure a good seal, and carefully place the lids and rims on.

5. Follow your boiling-water-bath canning process and process for 35 minutes, adjusting for altitude based on the chart on page 24.

apple juice

This is another big juice recipe that I'm sure seems like it might be excessive. It's not. It's a bit of a process to deal with chopping, cooking, and straining, so if you're going to do it, you might as well make a big batch. You'll love the outcome so much you will wish you had made a double batch.

MAKES 12–13 PINTS

Get your boiling-water-bath canning equipment ready and have your jars sterilized and ready.

25 pounds apples, preferably Fuji or Gala

8 cups water

$\frac{1}{2}$ cup fresh lemon juice

1. Core the apples and chop into 1" pieces, collecting the juices as you work. Transfer the apples and their juices to a large stainless steel pot, add the water, and bring to a boil over medium–high heat. Stir often and chop at the apples while you are stirring to help break them down. Reduce the heat to low and simmer, stirring and chopping frequently, for 30 to 45 minutes, or until the apples are almost mushy. Set aside for 30 minutes to cool.

2. Strain the apples through a fine strainer, sieve, or food mill set over a large pot or bowl. Let the pulp drain over the bowl for at least 2 hours to get as much juice as you can. Return the strained juice to the pot and add the lemon juice.

Increase the heat to medium and bring to a strong rolling boil. Make sure the temperature gets just over 190°F. Remove from the heat.

3. Carefully ladle or pour the hot juice into hot, sterilized jars, leaving $\frac{1}{4}$" of headspace. Gently tap the jars to remove air bubbles.

4. Wipe the rim of each jar carefully with a clean towel to ensure a good seal, and carefully place the lids and rims on.

5. Follow your boiling-water-bath canning process and process for 10 minutes, adjusting for altitude based on the chart on page 24.

juices and soups

vegetable broth

Vegetable broth, like all broths, is good to have on hand for all kinds of cooking needs. It can be a soup base, a flavoring for your pot of rice, and a seasoning for other vegetables. It's also a great low-fat substitute for oil in sautéing. I tend to save all my green vegetable scraps to throw in my broth pot, but this recipe is a good beginning guideline.

MAKES 7–8 QUARTS

Get your pressure-canning equipment ready and have your jars sterilized and ready.

2 tablespoons olive oil

4 sweet onions, roughly chopped

2 ribs celery, roughly chopped

½ cup fresh parsley, roughly chopped

20 cloves garlic, roughly chopped

3 tablespoons fresh basil, finely chopped

2 tablespoons fresh oregano, finely chopped

2 gallons water

5 pounds tomatoes, cored and roughly chopped

4 large bell peppers, cored and cut into strips

3 pounds carrots, cut into ½" slices

1 tablespoon kosher salt

½ tablespoon ground black pepper

1. Warm the oil in a large stainless steel pot over medium heat. Add the onions and celery and cook for 5 to 8 minutes, or until the onions are translucent. Add the parsley, garlic, basil, and oregano and cook for 1 minute. Stir in the water, tomatoes, bell peppers, carrots, salt, and pepper. Cover the pot and bring to a rolling boil. Reduce the heat to low and simmer, covered, for 6 to 8 hours, or until the broth has cooked down to the strength and flavor you want.

2. Strain the broth through a fine strainer, sieve, or food mill set over a large pot or bowl. Discard the solids.

3. Carefully ladle or pour the hot broth into hot, sterilized jars, leaving 1" of headspace. Gently tap the jars to remove air bubbles.

4. Wipe the rim of each jar carefully with a clean towel to ensure a good seal, and carefully place the lids and rims on.

5. Follow your pressure-canning process and process at 10 pounds of pressure for 1 hour 25 minutes, adjusting for altitude based on the chart on page 24.

juices and soups

vegetable soup

This is the basic vegetable soup I grew up with. It's the perfect representation of what's coming out of the garden in North Carolina at the end of July. When you can this, you get to open a jar of the perfect flavors of summer in the depth of December. One quart jar will give you 2 hearty dinner-size helpings.

MAKES 6–7 QUARTS

Get your pressure-canning equipment ready and have your jars sterilized and ready.

2 tablespoons olive oil

2 sweet onions, finely chopped

2 ribs celery, finely chopped

4 cloves garlic, finely chopped

3 tablespoons fresh basil, finely chopped

2 tablespoons fresh oregano, finely chopped

4 pounds tomatoes, cored and roughly chopped

2 pounds red potatoes, peeled and cut into $3/4$" cubes

2 pounds carrots, cut into $1/2$" slices

4 cups uncooked butterbeans

4 cups uncooked corn

6 cups water

1 teaspoon kosher salt

$1/2$ teaspoon ground black pepper

1. Warm the oil in a large stainless steel pot over medium heat. Add the onions and celery and cook for 5 to 8 minutes, or until the onions are translucent. Add the garlic, basil, and oregano and cook for 1 minute. Stir in the tomatoes, potatoes, carrots, beans, corn, water, salt, and pepper and bring to a rolling boil. Reduce the heat to medium-low and simmer for 10 minutes. Remove the pot from the heat.

2. Carefully use a ladle to evenly distribute the hot soup (solids and liquids) into hot, sterilized jars, leaving 1" of headspace. Gently tap the jars to remove air bubbles.

3. Wipe the rim of each jar carefully with a clean towel to ensure a good seal, and carefully place the lids and rims on.

4. Follow your pressure-canning process and process at 10 pounds of pressure for 1 hour 25 minutes, adjusting for altitude based on the chart on page 24.

CHAPTER 7

meat and fish

I'll be honest: Canning meat and fish was entirely foreign to me before I took on this book. While I have spent my entire life canning fruits and vegetables, meat and fish have always been something that I ate fresh or put in the freezer.

There are long and deep traditions in many cultures of canning meat and fish, and I have thoroughly enjoyed the process of learning these traditions. And let me be honest again: Canned spaghetti sauce with meat, ready to eat, is a game changer—a good, delicious dinner in no time. The canning option also helps save on tight freezer space.

Pay close attention to the instructions in these recipes. There is no room for substitutions here, so resist the urge to be creative. Botulism is no joke, so follow these recipes closely. Also, as with canning produce, use the freshest meat product you can find.

Note: When canning fish, sometimes white crystals form that look like salt or glass. It's totally normal. They are magnesium ammonium phosphate crystals and safe to eat. They usually melt away if you reheat the fish.

meat broth

This recipe is a little different from others in the book. Your yield will depend on the size and weight of the bones you use, what animal they are from, and how long they were roasted. In general, I use bones that I've roasted in normal recipes, so the bones aren't overcooked. Poultry bones do not need any extra preparation, but beef and pork bones will give a more flavorful broth if they are cracked or cut before you boil them.

YIELD VARIES BASED ON BATCH

Get your pressure-canning equipment ready and have your jars sterilized and ready.

Roasted bones, meat removed
1 tablespoon kosher salt per pound of bones

1. Rinse the bones and place in a large stainless steel pot. Add enough water to cover the bones by at least 1". Stir in the recommended amount of salt. Cover the pot and cook over high heat until it reaches a rolling boil. Reduce the heat to low and simmer, covered, for 3 to 4 hours, or until the broth has reach the desired consistency.

2. Strain the broth through a fine strainer, sieve, or food mill set over a large pot, and set the broth aside for 3 to 4 hours to fully cool. As it cools, the fat will rise to the top. Skim off and discard the fat (or refrigerate and use it for other recipes).

3. Return the pot of broth to the stovetop and bring to a rolling boil. As soon as it boils, remove it from the heat.

4. Carefully ladle or pour the hot broth into hot, sterilized jars, leaving 1" of headspace. Gently tap the jars to remove air bubbles.

5. Wipe the rim of each jar carefully with a clean towel to ensure a good seal, and carefully place the lids and rims on.

6. Follow your pressure-canning process and process at 10 pounds of pressure for 20 minutes for pint jars or 25 minutes for quart jars, adjusting for altitude based on the chart on page 24.

meat and fish

deboned meat

This recipe is a basic outline for canning deboned meat. It's almost impossible to give exact sizes and yield, because each animal's fat and moisture content vary drastically based on many different factors, so you have to adjust as you go. Be sure to have plenty of sterilized jars on hand. You can always rewash and reuse extra jars later if you prepared too many, but you cannot reheat the meat and start again if you prepared too few.

YIELD VARIES BASED ON BATCH

Get your pressure-canning equipment ready and have your jars sterilized and ready.

Raw meat, deboned and cut into 1" chunks or strips

Meat Broth (page 185), enough to cover the meat

2 tablespoons olive oil

1 tablespoon kosher salt per quart jar or 1/2 tablespoon per pint jar

1. Trim away any fat from the meat and discard (or save for a different recipe).

2. In a medium pot over high heat, bring the broth to a rolling boil.

3. Meanwhile, warm the oil in a large skillet over medium-high heat. Add the meat chunks and cook for 8 to 10 minutes, or until they are almost done: Poultry should be about two-thirds done and red meat should still be rare in the center.

4. Carefully put the hot meat chunks into hot, sterilized jars, add the recommended amount of salt per jar, and carefully ladle or pour the hot broth over the meat in each jar, leaving $1\frac{1}{4}$" of headspace. Make sure all the meat is covered with broth. Gently tap the jars to remove air bubbles.

5. Wipe the rim of each jar carefully with a clean towel to ensure a good seal, and carefully place the lids and rims on.

6. Follow your pressure-canning process and process at 10 pounds of pressure for 1 hour 15 minutes for pint jars or 1 hour 30 minutes for quart jars, adjusting for altitude based on the chart on page 24.

salmon and other fatty fish

This recipe is meant to be used with fatty fish like blues, mackerel, salmon, and steelhead trout instead of tuna. It's best to can fish that is fresh-caught. Make sure the fish was eviscerated within 2 hours after it was caught and was kept on ice until you canned it. Use the finished product to make fish cakes, croquettes, pasta sauces, or soups.

MAKES 4–5 PINTS

Get your pressure-canning equipment ready and have your jars sterilized and ready.

5–6 pounds fresh fish, skin on
1 teaspoon kosher salt per
    pint jar

1. Clean the fish really well, then remove the head, tail, fins, and scales. Rinse the fish again and make sure you have removed all the blood. Using a clean cutting board, cut the fish into slices 3½" long and 1" wide.
2. Pack the fish tightly, in standing rows with the skin side toward the glass, into hot, sterilized jars. Add the recommended amount of salt per jar. Leave 1" of headspace. Gently tap the jars to remove air bubbles. *Do not* add liquid to these jars.

3. Wipe the rim of each jar carefully with a clean towel to ensure a good seal, and carefully place the lids and rims on.
4. Follow your pressure-canning process and process at 10 pounds of pressure for 1 hour 40 minutes for pint jars, adjusting for altitude based on the chart on page 24.

tuna in oil

This was a product I was familiar with from living in Spain in college. I was thrilled to learn to make it at home. The tuna can be eaten straight from the jar as a snack or added to salads, pastas, and toasts for an added pungent twist.

When you are working with tuna, remember that it's a histamine fish and shouldn't be allowed to get warm until it is being cooked or processed. If the tuna isn't kept cold, it will start to break down and grow bacteria quickly. Always keep it on ice when you are working with it, and use the freshest fish you can get.

MAKES 4–5 HALF-PINTS

Get your pressure-canning equipment ready and have your jars ready.

3–4 pounds fresh tuna belly, skin on

$\frac{1}{2}$ teaspoon kosher salt per half-pint jar

2–3 cups olive oil

1. Preheat the oven to 350°F. Line a large baking pan with foil and place a cooking rack or grate in it.

2. Place the tuna belly skin side down on the prepared rack. Roast for 1 hour, then let cool on a rack on the counter for 1 hour. Cover tightly and refrigerate overnight.

3. The next day, take the tuna from the refrigerator, peel off the skin, and remove and discard any unsightly parts— blood vessels, bones, or discolored flesh. Slice the cleaned-up fish into $\frac{1}{4}$"-thick pieces that will fit lengthwise in your jars.

4. Pack the tuna tightly, in standing rows, into hot, sterilized jars. Add the recommended amount of salt per jar and pour enough of the oil into each jar to cover all the tuna. Leave 1" of headspace. Gently tap the jars to remove air bubbles.

5. Wipe the rim of each jar carefully with a clean towel to ensure a good seal, and carefully place the lids and rims on.

6. Follow your pressure-canning process and process at 10 pounds of pressure for 1 hour 40 minutes for pint or half-pint jars, adjusting for altitude based on the chart on page 24.

meat and fish

chili

This recipe is another brilliant time-saver. You'll have chili ready to go for hot dogs and hamburgers or as a simple meal on a cold winter night.

MAKES 4–5 QUARTS

Get your pressure-canning equipment ready and have your jars sterilized and ready.

3 cups dried beans (black, kidney, or pinto)

5 teaspoons kosher salt

2 pounds ground beef

1 pound ground pork

2 sweet onions, finely chopped

2 large bell peppers, cored and roughly chopped

4 cloves garlic, finely chopped

2 quarts canned tomatoes (page 40)

3 tablespoons chili powder

2 teaspoons smoked paprika

1 teaspoon ground black pepper

1. Place the beans and salt in a large stainless steel pot and add enough water to cover the beans by several inches. (Expect to use 3 cups of water for every cup of dried beans.) Bring the beans to a rolling boil and cook for 2 minutes. Remove from the heat and let the beans soak, covered, in the water for 1 hour. Drain the beans and return them to the pot.

2. Meanwhile, in a large skillet over medium-high heat, combine the beef, pork, onions, bell peppers, and garlic and cook for 8 to 10 minutes, or until the meat has browned. Drain the fat from the pan.

3. Transfer the meat mixture to the pot of beans and stir in the tomatoes, chili powder, paprika, and black pepper. Bring to a boil, stirring frequently to prevent sticking and to break down the tomatoes. Once it boils, immediately remove it from the heat.

4. Carefully ladle or pour the hot chili into hot, sterilized jars, leaving 1" of headspace. Gently tap the jars to remove air bubbles.

5. Wipe the rim of each jar carefully with a clean towel to ensure a good seal, and carefully place the lids and rims on.

6. Follow your pressure-canning process and process at 10 pounds of pressure for 1 hour 15 minutes, adjusting for altitude based on the chart on page 24.

spaghetti sauce

This is what I told you about at the beginning of the chapter. You're going to thank me for this when you've been at work all day, taken the kids to soccer, ballet, and tutoring, and then all you have to do to get dinner on the table is boil some noodles and open a jar of your homemade delicious meat sauce! You'll be a hero, and you'll have time for that much-needed glass of wine. Note that this recipe uses some of the Roasted Tomato Sauce you made over the summer, so you already have a head start.

MAKES 4–5 QUARTS

Get your pressure-canning equipment ready and have your jars sterilized and ready.

2 pounds ground beef

1 pound ground pork

5 cloves garlic, finely chopped

1 large bell pepper, cored and roughly chopped

1 pound button mushrooms, roughly chopped

2 pints Roasted Tomato Sauce (page 141)

¼ cup firmly packed light brown sugar

4 teaspoons kosher salt

2 teaspoons dried oregano

1 teaspoon dried basil

1 teaspoon ground black pepper

1. In a large skillet over medium-high heat, combine the beef, pork, garlic, bell pepper, and mushrooms and cook for 8 to 10 minutes, or until the meat has browned and the vegetables are tender. Drain the fat from the pan.

2. Transfer the meat mixture to a large pot and stir in the tomato sauce, sugar, salt, oregano, basil, and black pepper until well incorporated. Bring to a boil, reduce the heat to low, and simmer for 10 to 15 minutes, or until the sauce thickens to a spaghetti-sauce consistency—no longer runny, but not stiff enough that a spoon stands up.

3. Carefully ladle or pour the hot sauce into hot, sterilized jars, leaving 1" of headspace. Gently tap the jars to remove air bubbles.

4. Wipe the rim of each jar carefully with a clean towel to ensure a good seal, and carefully place the lids and rims on.

5. Follow your pressure-canning process and process at 10 pounds of pressure for 1 hour 15 minutes, adjusting for altitude based on the chart on page 24.

meat and fish

baked beans

These beans are so delicious. They can be a meal all to themselves. I'm not above eating them with a spoon straight from the jar, but they reheat in a snap and make a great quick side dish or option for a potluck or tailgate. I tend to make a double batch so that I heat up my kitchen making beans only once a season.

MAKES 7–8 QUARTS

Get your pressure-canning equipment ready and have your jars sterilized and ready.

5 pounds dried beans (black, kidney, cowpeas, or pinto)

5 tablespoons molasses or sorghum

2 tablespoons apple cider vinegar

2 tablespoons kosher salt

2 teaspoons dry mustard

2 teaspoons smoked paprika

1 pound bacon, cut into ½" pieces

1. Place the beans in a large stainless steel pot and add enough water to cover the beans by several inches. (Expect to use 3 cups of water for every cup of dried beans.) Bring the beans to a rolling boil and cook for 2 minutes. Remove from the heat and let the beans soak, covered, in the water for 1 hour.

2. Drain the beans over a large bowl, reserving the cooking water. Transfer the beans to a large ovenproof baking dish.

3. Preheat the oven to 350°F.

4. In a large mixing bowl, combine 4 cups of the reserved cooking water with the molasses or sorghum, vinegar, salt, mustard, and paprika. Mix well and pour over the beans in the baking dish. Scatter the bacon pieces on top, cover the dish, and bake for 3 to 4 hours, checking every hour: If the beans are drying out, add just enough liquid to cover the beans.

5. When the beans are soft, carefully ladle or pour the hot beans and liquid into hot, sterilized jars, leaving 1" of headspace. Gently tap the jars to remove air bubbles.

6. Wipe the rim of each jar carefully with a clean towel to ensure a good seal, and carefully place the lids and rims on.

7. Follow your pressure-canning process and process at 10 pounds of pressure for 1 hour 15 minutes, adjusting for altitude based on the chart on page 24.

ground meat

This recipe will come in useful if you have a hunter in the family and limited freezer space. You can grind up any meat like beef, venison, lamb, or pork; quickly brown it; and can it. To use, simply strain out the broth (save it for soups and seasonings) and reheat the meat on the stovetop. The meat makes a perfect filling for tacos or empanadas.

MAKES 4–5 PINTS

Get your pressure-canning equipment ready and have your jars sterilized and ready.

3 pints Meat Broth (page 185), enough to cover the meat

2 tablespoons olive oil

4 pounds ground meat

$\frac{1}{2}$ tablespoon kosher salt per pint jar

1. In a medium pot over high heat, bring the broth to a rolling boil.

2. Meanwhile, warm the oil in a large skillet over medium-high heat. Add the ground meat and cook for 8 to 10 minutes, or until the meat just starts to brown.

3. Carefully put the hot meat into hot, sterilized jars, add the recommended amount of salt per jar, and carefully ladle or pour the hot broth over the meat in each jar, leaving $1\frac{1}{4}$" of headspace. Make sure all the meat is covered with broth. Gently tap the jars to remove air bubbles.

4. Wipe the rim of each jar carefully with a clean towel to ensure a good seal, and carefully place the lids and rims on.

5. Follow your pressure-canning process and process at 10 pounds of pressure for 1 hour 15 minutes for pint jars, adjusting for altitude based on the chart on page 24.

meat and fish

salmon cakes

This recipe is for my mama. Salmon cakes are her comfort food—oddly enough, the thing her very Southern mother cooked and that my mama loved best. They are savory and satisfying.

MAKES 2–3 SERVINGS

½ cup all-purpose flour, plus
    more for dredging
2 small shallots, finely chopped
1 teaspoon dried dill
1 egg
1 pint canned salmon (page
    187), roughly chopped
Kosher salt and ground black
    pepper
Canola oil, for frying
Sour cream or crème fraîche,
    for serving

1. In a large bowl, vigorously whisk together the ½ cup flour, shallots, dill, and egg. Fold in the fish and mix until everything is incorporated. Refrigerate for 30 minutes, or until chilled and stiffened.

2. Shape the chilled fish mixture into patties, lay them on a flat surface, and use a sifter or strainer to lightly dust both sides with flour, salt, and pepper.

3. In a large cast-iron skillet over medium-high heat, heat ½" of oil until the oil is hot and sizzles when you drop a little flour in. Fry the fish cakes for 4 to 5 minutes on each side, using a metal spatula to carefully flip them, until the crust is golden brown. Transfer the fish cakes to paper towels to drain for a few minutes.

4. Serve warm with a little sour cream or crème fraîche for dipping.

shepherd's pie

This recipe uses chicken, so it is a lighter twist on the traditional shepherd's pie. You can use most any meat you like, even ground meat. Just be prepared for a runnier result if you incorporate ground meat.

MAKES 4–6 SERVINGS

1 unbaked piecrust

3 cups deboned canned chicken (page 186), drained

1 cup canned peas, drained (page 43)

1 cup sour cream

2 cups shredded Asiago cheese, divided

Kosher salt and ground black pepper

2 pints canned new potatoes (page 45), drained and mashed

1. Preheat the oven to 375°F.

2. Line a 9" deep-dish pie pan with the piecrust, making sure to stretch the crust over the rim of the pan.

3. In a large mixing bowl, combine the chicken, peas, sour cream, and 1 cup cheese. Season with salt and pepper to taste. Evenly spread the chicken mixture over the bottom of the pie pan. Evenly spread the mashed potatoes over the meat mixture and scatter remaining cheese, salt, and pepper over the top.

4. Bake, uncovered, for about 45 minutes, or until the cheese starts to bubble. Let the pie rest for 10 minutes before serving.

baked ziti

This recipes screams 1978, but it's just as delicious and easy to prepare now as it was then. You can make it with meat sauce or with a vegetarian option.

MAKES 4–6 SERVINGS

1 pound ziti pasta, cooked

4 cups ricotta cheese

4 cups shredded mozzarella cheese, divided

2 cups grated Parmesan cheese, divided

3 cups Spaghetti Sauce or Marinara Sauce (pages 193, 142)

Kosher salt and ground black pepper

1. Preheat the oven to 350°F.

2. In a large mixing bowl, combine the pasta, ricotta, 2 cups of the mozzarella, 1 cup of the Parmesan, and the sauce. Evenly spread this mixture into a 13" × 9" baking dish. Evenly top with the remaining 2 cups mozzarella and 1 cup Parmesan.

3. Bake uncovered for about 30 minutes, or until the cheese starts to bubble. Let the baked ziti rest for 10 minutes before serving.

CHAPTER 8

freeze these

This section is a collection of recipes that may have traditionally been canned but are now not recommended for canning in the home kitchen. There are lots of things you should not can at home, and most you can get along without. The recipes in this section are ones that keep my home happy and rolling along smoothly. I simply freeze them instead of canning.

Freezing requires much less equipment. You will still need your basic chopping and prepping equipment and a freezer to store things in, but you won't be boiling any jars here.

You can freeze in most canning jars if you leave enough headspace for the volume expansion that happens during freezing. Or you can freeze in freezer-safe plastic bags or containers. Make sure you date and label your containers so that you consume everything before freezer burn makes them inedible. The amount of time food can be frozen varies by product, but most things should be fine in your freezer for up to 6 months.

Caramel

Chimichurri

Chocolate
Sauce

Tahini

Pesto

Fall
Squash
Butter

pesto

Pesto is a magic ingredient in my kitchen. I put it on pasta and pizzas, in omelets and sandwiches, and dress all kinds of meat with it. You can freeze it in half-pint jars or, for smaller use, in ice cube trays. To use, just take out of the freezer and thaw on the counter for an hour.

MAKES 7–8 HALF-PINTS

Have your sterilized jars or plastic containers ready.

4 cups packed basil, arugula, or mizuna leaves

1 cup pecan or walnut pieces

1 cup freshly grated Parmesan cheese

6 cloves garlic, minced

1 teaspoon kosher salt, or more as needed

2 cups extra-virgin olive oil

1. In a food processor or high-powered mixer, combine the basil, nuts, Parmesan, garlic, and 1 teaspoon salt and pulse to blend. With the machine running, pour in the oil through the food tube in a slow, steady stream and process until smooth, stopping to scrape down the sides of the bowl as needed. Taste and adjust the salt as needed.

2. Spoon into sterilized containers and use immediately or store in the freezer. Leave $\frac{1}{2}$" of headspace if freezing.

chimichurri

I learned to make this divine herbal magic on a cattle farm in Argentina. The tangy herbal flavor is the perfect complement to a big juicy seared steak. It's also delicious on its own as a dipping sauce for bread or a condiment for a sandwich.

MAKES 4–5 HALF-PINTS

Have your sterilized jars or plastic containers ready.

4 cups fresh parsley

1 cup fresh cilantro

1 cup olive oil

$\frac{1}{3}$ cup red wine vinegar

6 cloves garlic

$\frac{1}{4}$ cup fresh lemon juice

1 teaspoon lemon peel

1 teaspoon kosher salt

$\frac{1}{2}$ teaspoon ground black pepper

$\frac{1}{2}$ teaspoon red-pepper flakes

1. In a food processor or high-powered mixer, combine the parsley, cilantro, oil, vinegar, garlic, lemon juice, lemon peel, salt, black pepper, and pepper flakes, pulsing a few times until the garlic is broken down but before a paste develops.

2. Transfer to sterilized containers and use immediately or store in the freezer. Leave $\frac{1}{2}$" of headspace if freezing.

freeze these

fall squash butter

Most folks think of apple, pear, or pumpkin butters, but all fall squash can be treated just like pumpkins. So if you've got some butternuts or a giant blue Hubbard sitting around, get to roasting, and you'll have a sweet treat hiding in your freezer all winter long. A squash butter holds up better to freezing than canning because the flesh is so dense that canning doesn't get the ingredients hot enough for proper storage. This freezer version is delicious and thaws quickly. You can also treat it like a granita and shave it into pieces for a dessert. Just top with whipped cream, and you are a gourmand!

MAKES 4 PINTS

Have your sterilized jars or plastic containers ready.

5 pounds fall squash (butternut, acorn, or Hubbard)

1 cup firmly packed dark brown sugar

1/4 cup apple cider, plus more as needed

4 tablespoons molasses or sorghum

1 teaspoon grated fresh ginger

1 tablespoon ground cinnamon

1/2 teaspoon ground nutmeg

1 teaspoon fresh lemon juice

1 teaspoon vanilla extract

1/2 teaspoon kosher salt

1. Preheat the oven to 400°F.

2. Slice the squash in half and remove the seeds (save those seeds to roast later!). Place the halves on a roasting pan, skin side up, and roast for 30 to 45 minutes, or until the squash is nearly fork-tender. Transfer the pan to a rack and let the squash fully cool. Peel off and discard the skin, and slice the squash into smaller pieces.

3. In a food processor or high-powered blender, combine the squash, sugar, cider, molasses or sorghum, ginger, cinnamon, and nutmeg, processing until smooth.

4. Transfer the mixture to a medium pot over medium heat. Cover with a splatter guard and bring to a low boil, stirring frequently. Reduce the heat to low and simmer, still stirring, for 15 to 30 minutes (depending on the moisture in the squash), or until you've reached the desired consistency. Remove from the heat and stir in the lemon juice, vanilla, and salt.

5. Spoon into containers and use immediately, store in the fridge for up to 2 weeks, or put away in the freezer. Leave 1/2" of headspace if freezing.

tahini

Tahini is a wonderful ingredient to have on hand. It's an integral part of many Mediterranean dishes but is often expensive to buy from the supermarket. It's super-easy to make at home and thaws quickly at room temperature.

MAKES 3–4 HALF-PINTS

Have your sterilized jars or plastic containers ready.

4 cups hulled sesame seeds
1 cup light olive oil
1 teaspoon kosher salt

1. In an extra-large skillet over medium-low heat, toast the sesame seeds by stirring them constantly for 3 to 5 minutes, or until the seeds just begin to change color but have not turned brown. You'll start to smell the rich roasted smell. Immediately remove them from the heat and pour them onto a large cold pan or cutting board. Spread them in a thin layer to cool completely.

2. Pour the cooled seeds into a food processor or high-powered blender and process until a paste forms. Slowly pour in a small amount of the oil and process to incorporate. Once the first bit is completely mixed in, slowly drizzle in the rest of the oil with the processor or blender running, and process until the tahini is fully mixed and satiny in texture. Add $\frac{1}{2}$ teaspoon of the salt, pulse once, and taste. Add the remaining $\frac{1}{2}$ teaspoon salt if you think it needs more, and pulse one more time.

3. Spoon into sterilized containers and use immediately, store in the fridge for up to 2 weeks, or put away in the freezer. Leave $\frac{1}{2}$" of headspace if freezing.

freeze these

chocolate sauce

This chocolate fudge sauce is a lifesaver when you have unexpected guests. You can throw together a delicious dessert in minutes by quickly thawing this sauce in a double boiler on the stove top or by microwaving it (remove the container lid first!) for a few 10-second intervals. You'll have sundae and cake topping in no time.

MAKES 2–3 HALF-PINTS

Have your sterilized jars or plastic containers ready.

24 ounces semisweet chocolate chips
$2/_3$ cup heavy cream
$1/_2$ cup (1 stick) unsalted butter
1 teaspoon cornstarch
$1/_2$ teaspoon ground cinnamon
1 teaspoon vanilla extract

1. In a medium heatproof bowl or the top pan of a double boiler, combine the chocolate chips, cream, butter, cornstarch, and cinnamon. If using a bowl, place it over a medium pot half-filled with water. If using a double boiler, add water to the lower pan and set the smaller one on top. Cook over medium-high heat, stirring occasionally with a whisk. When the chocolate starts to melt after about 5 minutes, stir more frequently.

2. When the chocolate is completely melted, move the top container from the double-boiler setup to the counter. Add the vanilla and whisk vigorously until everything is smooth and perfectly blended.

3. Spoon into containers and use immediately, store in the fridge for a few days, or put away in the freezer. Leave $1/_2$" of headspace if freezing.

caramel

Caramel is another sweet lifesaver. It can be anything from a sundae topping to a filler in cakes or pies. To use after freezing, thaw overnight in the refrigerator or heat gently on the stovetop.

MAKES 2–3 HALF-PINTS

Have your sterilized jars or plastic containers ready.

2 cups firmly packed light
    brown sugar
1 cup heavy cream
1/2 cup (1 stick) unsalted butter
1 tablespoon vanilla extract
1/2 teaspoon kosher salt

1. In a medium stainless steel pot over medium-high heat, combine the sugar, cream, butter, vanilla, and salt, stirring gently with a whisk. The sugar will bubble up and cook down. After the bubbles have cooked down, about 5 minutes, stir until the sauce is as thick as you want and remove from the heat.

2. Spoon into containers and use immediately, store in the fridge for a few days, or put away in the freezer. Leave 1/2" of headspace if freezing.

pesto and blue cheese pasta

This sounds like a random combination and was an accidental one, but after the first accident, I've been making this recipe over and over again. The green flavors of the pesto pair beautifully with the earthy blue cheese, and the vinegar in the cherry tomatoes is a great contrast to the fat from the bacon.

MAKES 4 SERVINGS

½ pound bacon, sliced in
    ½" pieces
1 pint Pickled Cherry Tomatoes
    (page 103), drained
1 pound fettuccine pasta,
    cooked
1 half-pint pesto (page 206)
1 cup strong blue cheese (like a
    Stilton), crumbled

1. In a large cast-iron skillet over medium heat, cook the bacon until almost brown. Transfer the bacon to a plate.
2. Add the cherry tomatoes to the pan and quickly toss to heat and coat them with bacon fat.
3. Add the cooked pasta, pesto, and bacon and stir to coat. Scatter the blue cheese on top and serve immediately.

freeze these

seared steaks with chimichurri

Argentina's most perfect meal, with flavors straight from your freezer. If you have extra sauce, use it as a bread dipping sauce or a dressing for roasted potatoes.
MAKES 4 SERVINGS

2 tablespoons olive oil
2 tablespoons kosher salt
1 tablespoon ground black
    pepper
4 steaks (rib eye, New York
    strip, filet mignon), 1"
    thick
1 cup Chimichurri (page 207)

1. In a small bowl, combine the oil, salt, and pepper. Rub the mixture evenly over the steaks. Set the steaks aside for 20 minutes to rest.

2. Coat a grill rack with cooking spray. For a charcoal grill, prepare one dense layer of hot coals. For a gas grill, preheat until the grates are good and hot.

3. Grill the steaks for 3 to 5 minutes on each side, or until a thermometer inserted in the center registers 145°F for medium-rare. You'll have a nice sear on the outside and a moist pink center.

4. Let the steaks rest for a few minutes before serving and dress with a heaping spoonful of the chimichurri sauce on top of each one.

caramel pear tart

This is a lovely dessert for fall dinners, even at Thanksgiving. The caramel adds decadence, and the pears help lighten the mood.

MAKES 4–6 SERVINGS

1 unbaked piecrust

2 pints canned pears (page 34), drained and thinly sliced

½ teaspoon ground cinnamon

1 pint caramel (page 211)

¼ cup fresh mint, roughly chopped

2 tablespoons molasses

1. Preheat the oven to 375°F. Line a 9" pie pan with the piecrust.

2. Place the pears in a bowl and toss with the cinnamon.

3. Spread the caramel evenly in the pie shell. Place the pear slices in a spiral pattern on top of the caramel. Sprinkle the chopped mint over the pears, then drizzle molasses in thin lines over the entire tart.

4. Bake for 15 to 20 minutes, or until the tart's edges and pears are golden brown. Let the tart sit for at least 15 minutes before slicing and serving.

freeze these

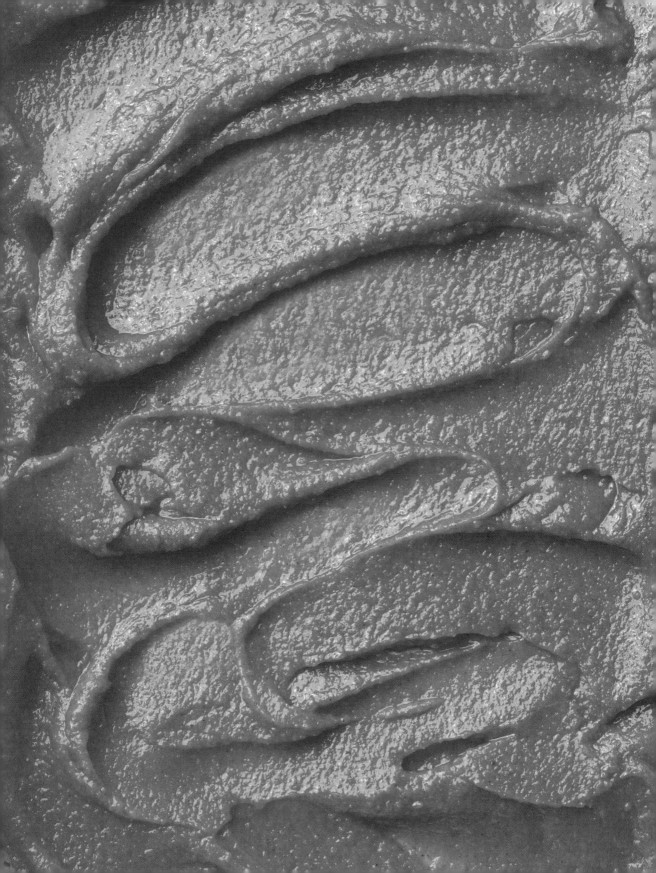

acknowledgments

THE ACKNOWLEDGMENTS FOR THIS BOOK ARE A LITTLE UNUSUAL. Many of the people I need to thank are no longer with us. When I talk to people about the way I cook, I always go back to how I grew up and people regularly comment that it sounds like I'm from a time-warped kitchen. My family really did can and freeze obsessively. We sat shelling peas and butterbeans on Saturday nights, watching *Fantasy Island,* so we could can them on Sunday afternoons. The lessons I learned then are the ones I used to write this book.

So, I need to start by thanking the women who shaped my life from the very beginning—my mama, both grandmothers, my great-grandmother, great-aunts, cousins, and family friends. I love food and cooking traditions because of all of you.

Thank you to the amazing team at Rodale Books for taking *Canning* and turning it into a work of art. Thank you to my phenomenal editor, Dervla Kelly, for having the vision for a new book on an old subject; to Anna Cooperberg for answering every question and keeping me on track; and to Yeon Kim and team for making jam and pickles look like fine art.

Thank you to my wise and wonderful agent, Leslie Stoker, for constant support, the most helpful feedback, and diligent outreach on my behalf.

Thank you to the marathon list of friends and family, at Coon Rock Farm and around the world, who have helped roast tomatoes or pickle scallions, and fill jars, and stick on labels over the years. All that practice contributed to this gorgeous book.

And, as always, thank you, Richard, for tasting all the best bites of life with me. You make every day better.

index